IS ANYBODY OUT THERE?

IS ANYBODY OUT THERE?
THE NEW BLUEPRINT FOR MARKETING COMMUNICATIONS
IN THE 21ST CENTURY

MARK AUSTIN & JIM AITCHISON

John Wiley & Sons (Asia) Pte Ltd

To Kate, Max, Alice, Olivia and Annabelle,
my shining stars, with love.

Mark Austin

To my media queens,
Ginette and Elise, with love.

Jim Aitchison

Published in 2003 by John Wiley & Sons (Asia) Pte Ltd
2 Clementi Loop, #02-01, Singapore 129809

Other Wiley Editorial Offices

John Wiley & Sons, Inc., 605 Third Avenue, New York, NY 10158-0012, USA
John Wiley & Sons Ltd, Baffins Lane, Chichester West Sussex PO191 UD, England
John Wiley & Sons (Canada) Ltd, 22 Worcester Road, Rexdale, Ontario M9W 1L1, Canada
John Wiley & Sons Australia Ltd, 33 Park Road (PO Box 1226),
Milton, Queensland 4046, Australia
Wiley-VCH, Pappelallee 3, 69469 Weinham, Germany

Library of Congress Cataloging-in-Publication Data:

ISBN 0-470-82055-1

Typeset in 12.5/17.5 point, Bauer Bodoni, by WORK
Printed in Singapore by Saik Wah Press Pte Ltd
10 9 8 7 6 5 4 3 2 1

CONTENTS

AUTHORS' NOTES

Media and creative — the main two functions of the full service advertising agency business, kept apart for so long, but always with so much that is complementary.

There is a great deal written and debated about how the advertising and marketing services industry generally has lost its way, how it has allowed itself to become outmoded and disconnected from the commercial reality of brands, the ever evolving behaviour of people (normally known as consumers) and the massive impact of technology on the channels that connect them. Brand owners generally have one consistent goal: growth. And this book is all about how, in the context of this brave new world, by working in partnership with brand owners and the full range of marketing specialists, growth can be achieved.

It is not insignificant that this book has been written by a media man in partnership with one of the most highly respected creative brains in Asia. It signifies the potential of finding the right way in this day and age to reunite these crucial functions to deliver growth. After all, growth is the only option — both professionally and personally.

MARK AUSTIN
SINGAPORE 2003

To my knowledge, this is the first book ever written by a media man and a creative man. (And definitely the first with a media man as passionate and visionary as Mark Austin.) As such, it deserves some explanation.

Jean-Marie Dru, my great advertising icon, once quoted from a book called *Built to Last*. The quote was all about "The Tyranny of the Or", in which the authors challenged conventional thinking that says it is impossible to be two things at the same time. You have to choose. You have to be either, or… If you are a star striker in soccer, you can't be a great defender. If you are creative, you can't be strategic. Sadly, we are conditioned to think like that. Jean-Marie's point was that we should transcend such conventions.

In advertising, creative people cannot simply be creative people, locked away in our own little world, shielded from some rather ugly realities. Our industry has changed beyond recognition in the last decade. Our clients now expect different things from us. Like it or not, we create within a different context. We have to think creatively and strategically. We have to understand the new ways that consumers consume media (and therefore consume our work). We have to engage our minds with the effects that brands, consumers and media channels have on each other, and on our creativity. We have to be more business-driven. We have to understand the other disciplines in our industry, and what is happening within our industry, and why it is happening. If we want people in our industry to listen to our opinions, our opinions have to be better informed.

If we believe in advertising, if we believe in creativity, if we have a passion to do great creative work, we have to understand where and how we fit into this new, complex, and yes, frightening world of marketing communications. It is no longer just about doing a great 30-seconder. It is no longer just about doing a great print ad. It is about applying our talent with more meaning, more relevance, and with greater effect, over a much broader canvas.

JIM AITCHISON
SINGAPORE 2003

ACKNO

Our sincere thanks to everyone who contributed their time, insights and talent to our book, especially David Mayo, Richard Armstrong and the brilliant team at Red Card Singapore; Martin Raymond and Chris Sanderson of The Future Laboratory London; Patrick Low, executive creative director DY&R Singapore; and for his extraordinary support, Thomas Ang, general manager of Comfort Ads.

Our special thanks to Theseus Chan, who designed and produced this book, and his team Andie Ngoh and Evonne Ng at WORK Singapore for their care and craft. And to Johnson Tan at ProColor Singapore for his skill and dedication.

To Nick Wallwork, Publisher, at John Wiley & Sons (Asia), and our editors Malar Manoharan and Grace Pundyk, our warm gratitude for their patience and guidance throughout the project.

MARK AUSTIN & JIM AITCHISON

LEDGMENTS

The most important person to thank for her wonderful support, understanding and encouragement in the production of this book is my amazing wife, Kate. Thanks, darling, couldn't have done it without you.

I am most fortunate to work with some of the brightest, most visionary people in our business. Far smarter than I, they have been able to turn ideas and notions into a wonderfully invigorating, creative and actionable process.

In this regard, my thanks to Mark Sherrington who put massive amounts of unsung energy into making communications channel planning a reality; and to Julia Singleton, Mel Varley and Martin Thomas, whose intellect, guidance, honesty and inspiration have been invaluable.

My thanks also to my colleague, Mainardo de Nardis, for encouraging me to complete this project and to Wendy Robertson, Lea Gregory and Catherine Potter for all their help. I am indebted to my friend and fellow author Ken Sacharin for allowing me access to his far better brain. Last but not least, to my friend Little Otto, for whom everything until now has been satisfactory.

MARK AUSTIN

PRESENT
IMPERFECT

Chapter 1

CONFLUENCE OF CHANGE

Most marketing programmes are based on the fear that the market might see what's really going on inside the company.
THE CLUETRAIN MANIFESTO

Consumers are immune to marketing. Virtually every great brand is now in decline. And the advertising agencies that built them are dinosaurs on the verge of extinction.

Hype or reality? We are in the third decade of a multidimensional confluence of change. Change driven by revolutionary developments in consumer behaviour and attitudes, by newly emerging communications channels, and fuelled by inexorable developments in technology. The successful marketers will be those who understand how those changes began, where they will eventually carry us, and how we should respond to them.

Those Were The Days

Historically, communicating brands to consumers had been relatively simple and cost effective. For example, in the early 1980s a peak spot in *Coronation Street* would regularly deliver 50% or more of all TV-owning homes in the UK. All a marketer had to do was instruct his advertising agency to do an ad, buy some big rating spots and a few others earlier and later to boost the campaign's frequency, and the job was done.

The whole family sat in front of the TV, watching in

a non-interactive, habitual way. They did not have remote controls. A marketer could reach pretty much the whole adult population easily and cheaply. In every market around the world there would be two, at most three choices of TV channel. In the UK, a home would be either an ITV or a BBC home. Often the channel would not change the whole night. The audiences were enormous, very loyal to the programmes, absorbing — and crucially, believing — the information they received. Big brands were sending big messages out to big audiences. "As seen on TV" became the catchwords of brand quality. Mass media delivering mass audiences played a key role in helping to build mass brands. **Today, with very few exceptions, this dynamic has ceased to exist.**

Given that context, the single most important issue affecting a brand's growth was the quality of the creative execution of a television commercial. For many successful brands, the TV commercial itself was effectively "The Brand Strategy", not just for advertising communications but often for the whole brand positioning across the complete spectrum of target audiences — including the retail trade. But with so much change about to happen, with so many conventional dynamics being challenged, it would not be the case for much longer.

Fast-Forward
The evolution of media channels, the arrival of the TV remote control, and the emergence of a more independently minded, better educated consumer all happened around the same time.

The advent of video, mobile telephony, computers, computer games and the World Wide Web changed forever the dynamic of the family sitting in front of the box. Audiences soon began to divide their time between these different technologies, and usually in different locations within the home. Armed with the ultimate consumer weapon — the TV remote control — audiences could wage war against big boring brand messages. Today, American adman Andy Berlin says advertising has to be "a transaction: an exchange of attention for a reward". A zapper combined with PC technology and hard drives can pause a "live" TV programme so that "you can eat dinner, or make love, or go to the bathroom. You can fast forward thirty seconds and skip the commercial. Unless that commercial is so good that people want to watch it, *it simply won't be watched.*"

Technology drove the speed of change, which in turn caused audiences to change and fragment even faster. At the same time, consumers became increasingly aware of their value to brand owners. And they were starting to engage in an activity that they had been surprisingly reticent to do before. When they were not happy, they were starting to complain, to demand their money back if they were not satisfied, and to tell their family and friends all about it as well. They understood that they had choices, and that there were alternatives, and they were becoming increasingly prepared to reappraise their brand loyalties. Around this time, somewhat amusingly, marketers coined the phrase "brand promiscuity" to define this new phenomenon of consumers switching brands, as though they were some errant adolescents daring to challenge the parental authority of brands.

The developments in technology also drove the proliferation of media channels. More conventional media appeared. More TV stations, terrestrial, satellite and cable. More newspapers and magazines penetrated every market. And more new media channels emerged: the World Wide Web, MP3, mobile phones and computer games. By the end of the century marketers had begun the game of tag, desperately trying to catch the increasingly elusive consumer. Soon brand messages were springing up everywhere, often in new guises. Conventional media offered new options — increased sponsorships, product placements and celebrity endorsements. Unconventional platforms arrived on the scene. Words like "buzz", "viral" and "womb" started to be heard in marketing circles.

CONSUMERS, CHANNELS AND BRANDS DRIVEN BY TECHNOLOGY

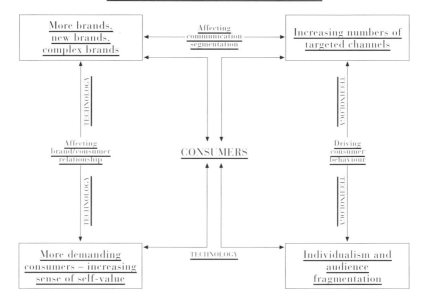

The end result: information overload, or as the anti-marketing extremists term it, **"marketing pollution"**. In *Attention!* Ken Sacharin observed: "It's gotten to the point that media are being considered pollution. Information is piling up like garbage. And the irony of our information age is that as we collectively try to rise above the noise, we end up creating more of it."

As a result of this clutter, consumers are "commercials veterans", bombarded with up to 1,500 messages a day. In *Under the Radar*, Jonathan Bond and Richard Kirshenbaum noted: "Consumers are like roaches. We spray them with marketing, and for a time it works. Then, inevitably, they develop an immunity, a resistance."

Consumers have no alternative but try to avoid the message missiles aimed at them. Sacharin points out that as marketers try to break through consumer defence mechanisms, all they do is create more noise pollution that generates even more message avoidance: a vicious and unprofitable circle. As the 74th Thesis of *The Cluetrain Manifesto* puts it from the consumer's perspective: "We are immune to advertising. Just forget it."

Managing communications in this increasingly complex scenario demands **a thorough understanding of the inter- and intra-relationships between consumers, communication channels and brands**: the effects of channels on consumer behaviour and attitudes, the effects of consumer behaviour on marketing and brand activity, and the effects of channels on how marketers communicate their brands to consumers.

Chapter 2

BRANDS UNDER THREAT

I picture the reality in which we live in terms of a military occupation. We are occupied the way the French and Norwegians were occupied by the Nazis during World War II, but this time by an army of marketers. We have to reclaim our country from those who occupy it on behalf of their global masters.

URSULA FRANKLIN, PROFESSOR EMERITUS, UNIVERSITY OF TORONTO

Taken from Naomi Klein's *No Logo*, Franklin's somewhat extreme point of view nonetheless posts a potent warning to marketers. Globally, there is a growing backlash against what is seen as the exploitation of societies for the commercial gain of corporations.

Marketing Backlash

For this growing band of anti-marketers, spurred on by books such as Klein's *No Logo*, antipathy to marketing has become almost spiritual. Klein herself was rated one of the world's most influential people under 35 by the *London Times*. She argued that people are living in a "brandscape", the subjects of a "sponsored world", their lives controlled by powerful, insidious brands. Companies no longer produce products, she alleges; they market corporate brand images, aspirations and lifestyles, infiltrating and manipulating every aspect of our social structure from the education of our children, through to the content of our entertainment and the shape of our high streets and shopping malls.

Are brands really that powerful? Is the public so easily manipulated? *The Economist* (8 September, 2001) suggested a more complicated, if gentler reality: "Many of the established brands that top the league tables are in trouble, losing customer loyalty and value." Names like Kellogg's, Kodak, Marlboro and Nescafé are no longer in the top 10. According to brand consultancy Interbrand, Kellogg's was in second place less than a decade ago — today it has slipped to 39th position. Of the 74 brands in the top 100 league in both 2000 and 2001, 41 declined in value in the space of a year. As well, the combined value of the 74 brands fell by US$49 billion, an unsettling 5%.

The concept of a "brand" is in transition. Only a few years ago, brands were universally viewed as invaluable by manufacturing and service businesses alike. Former Coca-Cola chief marketing officer Sergio Zyman said: "A brand is a company's ultimate asset. It invests an otherwise generic product or service with a meaning that goes beyond the product itself." Today, the view is not so clear and there is a range of opinion among brand owners themselves. On one hand, Unilever chairman Niall FitzGerald believes "a brand is a storehouse of trust", and Nestlé's chief Peter Brabeck argues that "in technocratic and colourless times, brands bring warmth, familiarity and trust". On the other, Disney chairman Michael Eisner describes the word brand as "overused, sterile and unimaginative".

A recent survey of a number of leading European

companies discovered that **the boards of many large corporations spend less than 1% of their time discussing marketing**.

This was further substantiated by the London Business School's Tim Ambler whose 30-month research project among leading UK brand-owning corporations revealed that **company boards pay nine times more attention to counting and spending cash flow than worrying where it comes from**. Ambler's findings went on to establish that while company boards favour marketing as a broad concept, they are confused about brands and brand equity. This led to the general lack of interest shown by most boards towards their brands. As Ambler ruefully observed, chief financial officers shared the illusion that "the more often you count a pile of money, the bigger it gets". He argued logically that while the value of brands or brand equity does not appear on a company's books, it is by far their most valuable asset and should be regularly assessed to truly understand the company's performance. At the very least, he urged, major businesses need to consider brand equity in terms of three audiences: the employees of the company, the direct or trade customers, and the ultimate end user — the consumer. Ambler predicted that by 2010, all well-managed businesses will be appraising their brands once or twice a year. But for now, confusion reigns in the boardroom and counting the money is the priority.

The Fear Factor

Not surprisingly, all these issues have made marketing

decision-makers increasingly insecure, a syndrome exacerbated by procurement officers who have become more involved in marketing investment decisions generally, and advertising decisions specifically. Everything has to be measured quantitatively. Like never before, brand owners are looking at what media coverage they are gaining, what discounts they are getting, and what advertising agency fees or commissions they are paying.

The rise of procurement specialists signals a major restructure of advertising practices. Once, company procurement officers purchased consumables at minimum cost mainly through the tendering process. Now their gaze passes across *every* aspect of business, says David Baker, former CEO and co-founder of Australian media specialist Advertising Investment Services (AIS), now Starcom. Basing assumptions on savings achieved in other activities, some businesses will set savings targets of up to 20% on total advertising costs over three to five years, but still anticipate the same advertising effectiveness. Procurement officers, says Baker, consider media costs are too high. Seeking improved efficiencies, they are scrutinising the relationship between company marketing people and marketing services suppliers. Baker foreshadows a "new client whose objectives, service requirements, and dimension of pricing arrangements for services, are likely to differ from those we have been accustomed to for many years". Notice has been served.

Yet, despite all advice to the contrary, few marketers are looking as hard as they should be at innovation, at breaking out of a "price-first" mentality and trying to

bust conventions. If anything, everything has to be more and more measurable. Creativity has been stymied, risk and imagination stifled.

Even consistency, the factor underpinning many great brands, has been compromised. The average job tenure of a marketing director in Britain has slipped to as little as 12 to 15 months, less in Asia. Each new appointee earnestly sets about putting his or her stamp on brand culture. As a result, brand building has become, at best, erratic. The tragedy is that the soul of the brand, and the permanence and reassurance it once offered consumers in an uncertain world, are jeopardised.

Marketers today are more concerned than ever about failure and this in turn causes short-termism. "Is it going to be successful?" is a recurring question. Yet curiously the majority of companies in Asia, for example, cite cost pressures as the reason why they inadequately invest in measuring their return on marketing investment. Their objectives, too, can often be as woolly as "We want to increase awareness", or "We want to increase sales". But in order to answer questions like "Where are you now?" or "Where do you want to be?" tracking studies are too infrequently entertained, especially in Asia. Clearly, if they don't know where they are or where they want to be, getting from one point to another will be reminiscent of *Alice in Wonderland*. When Alice asked the Mad Hatter for directions, he asked her: "Where do you want to go?" Alice replied, "I'm not really sure," to which the Mad Hatter said, "Well then, it doesn't matter which way you go."

On the other hand, Western companies have a huge

IS ANYBODY OUT THERE?

amount of evidence to support marketing communications investments and historically have been extremely successful at building brands all over the world. With one or two exceptions like Singapore Airlines, Western companies are much better at building brands in Asia than Asian companies building brands in Asia. The biggest hurdle for many Asian companies is their trading mentality and its resultant short-termism. It has served them well for generations, but brand building is a new discipline in Asia requiring a different level of sophistication. Their experience in the qualitative aspects of brand building is limited.

To fear can be added frustration. Marketing executives in Asia, Australia and other outposts of brand empires are increasingly affected by the inexorable trend towards globalisation. Global advertising campaigns are imposed on them by head office. So, too, are international agency alignments. The opportunities for them to pioneer new strategies and develop fresh communications tailored to the often vastly different markets and cultures of Asia are diminishing. They learn the disciplines of marketing, but have little opportunity to practise them. Which in turn contributes to Asia's lack of experienced homegrown marketers and perpetuates the *status quo* of Asian brands vis-à-vis their Western counterparts.

Dysfunctional Brand Building

Steve Henry of Howell Henry Chaldecott Lury, a leading London advertising agency, said that brands are arguably the biggest thing in the world, bigger even than organised religion or politics. Andy Berlin said: "People use brands as furniture to decorate their realities and help make them more real, more satisfying." Jonathan Bond and Richard Kirshenbaum defined brands as "communities of users" — the Apple Mac community, the Mercedes-Benz community, the Harley-Davidson community — with users bonded together globally by the values and spirit of the brand.

Once, brand owners created messages that defined their brands to consumers. Now we have entered a brave new world. The power has shifted. Today, consumers define brands by choosing how they wish to interpret them. The people who actually use the brand will ultimately decide what the brand is and what it stands for. Thus, in Naomi Klein's thought camp, the Nike "Swoosh" stands more for a corporation with child labour issues than it does for *Just do it*. And because brands exist only in the minds of the users, it will be they who define a brand's success, not the marketer.

In other words, brand owners have seen control of their brands pass to consumers.

In fact, today's consumer will often redefine brands, whether a marketer likes it or not. A good case of this was given in Malcolm Gladwell's insightful book *The Tipping Point*. Hush Puppies, popular in the 1960s and 70s, were being sold off in the shops in Greenwich Village, New York. When some style leaders decided that they were quite cool, that the 60s culture was coming back, everyone else started buying them. The consumer had decided that desert boots were trendy again. In other cases where brands had been positioned in a certain way, consumers had found new, unplanned values in them.

Understandably enough, many brand owners view this development with a degree of apprehension. Others see it as a new and dramatic opportunity.

Advertising's Role In Brand Building

For decades, advertising was the mainstay of successful brand building. Today clients everywhere seem to have deprioritised advertising both in terms of marketing investment and in relation to its influence on their overall business strategy.

It used to be that Charles and Maurice Saatchi would talk to Prime Minister Margaret Thatcher. Their partnership resulted in highly creative campaigns that played a significant role in winning elections. While that was indicative of the power of advertising then, it is far from the case today.

The reality now is that advertising is not as high on the agenda as it used to be. In fact, it is increasingly rare that a senior advisory relationship will exist between an agency CEO and a client CEO. Once, the head of an agency was one of the closest advisers to the chairman or CEO of a client company. It gave agencies the ultimate level of influence in shaping the destiny of a brand. Then came the advent of client marketing departments and brand consultants. Given advertising's diminished role and therefore its contribution to a company's success, the individuals who run those agencies have consequently diminished in influence with senior client management.

Nor in this communications age does it help the manufacturers' cause when famous brands are exposed for anti-social activities. Consumers are challenging the relevance and desirability of brands *per se*, their role in society, and the dissonance that exists between the outward expression of a corporation through its advertised brands and the reality of what they really are. In *The Cluetrain Manifesto*, the implications for marketers are clearly stated: "Companies need to realise that their markets are often laughing. At them."

Nearly half of all American college students have taken marketing courses. They have been educated in the art of deconstructing commercials so that every claim, every nuance, can be scrutinised and evaluated. For younger, more cynical audiences, shooting down advertising has become a consumer sport.

Driven by technology, the explosion of media channels and the resultant change in consumer behaviour and attitudes have reshaped the marketing communications landscape. Brand owners themselves are caught in this maelstrom of uncertainty and have not escaped the fast changing dynamics. Yet while communications channels and consumers have changed beyond recognition, by and large marketing has not. "Marketing," alleges author Elliott Ettenburg, "is stuck in the past."

"Is My Advertising Working?"

Advertising is blamed for every sin under the sun. All too often the advertising was wrong and doomed to fail, or too much was expected of it.

Frequently, advertising is tasked with achieving the wrong objective — for example, increasing awareness. "Increasing awareness" looks good on paper, but what does it actually mean? Awareness is a passive emotion. It means that consumers will be aware of the brand, but nothing more. **A lift in awareness does not automatically lead to a lift in sales.**

When Andrew Ehrenberg researched the relationship between advertising and consumer behaviour in the supermarket, he found that awareness was not a highly emotional state, nor did it imply an active predisposition to buy the brand. He said that the trigger to purchase was more likely to come from the external world — a cut-price offer or an in-store demonstration — than from the internal world of attitudes and dispositions. Along with psychologist Leon Festinger (author of *A Theory of Cognitive Dissonance*) and Dr. Herbert Krugman, Ehrenberg concluded that advertising's main role is reinforcing feelings of satisfaction with brands already bought.

In his book *The End of Advertising As We Know It*, Sergio Zyman also argued that "**Awareness doesn't sell.** All it does is get you into the consideration set. And then you still have to sell." According to Zyman, "Traditional advertising doesn't work and companies who don't get wise to this are going to fail… Awareness — which is what most ads are designed to increase — doesn't get you sales."

Another fallacy: marketers frequently advertise with the objective of changing consumer attitudes in order to change consumer behaviour. The theory is flawed. As Festinger indicated, attitudes tend to be the result of behaviour, not the cause of it. Krugman's research into advertising reached a similar finding: identifiable attitude change occurs after the purchase and not before it.

Thus, attitudes are significant only when tied to experience.

The role of advertising has often been defined as changing, modifying or affirming consumer behaviour. A marketer's objectives might be to persuade consumers to try a new product, to keep buying an existing product, to use the product more often, or to use the product in a new way. Certainly, awareness will be a by-product of the advertising, not its central motivation. **But in this day and age of consumer cynicism and knowledge, is it realistic to expect that this can still be the case?**

Among the most disquieting research findings of recent years, Ehrenberg — together with Neil Barnard and John Scriven at London's South Bank University — challenged the more traditional views of advertising.

Brand advertising does not work by persuading consumers that a brand is different or better than similar ones. Nor does advertising invest the brand with intangible, emotional "added values" that motivate consumers. Advertising, they argued, leaves and reinforces longer-term memory traces and added associations for the brand. In their view, advertising should focus on increasing the profitable number of people who see the brand as salient to them, as a brand they might buy. But it does not function by persuasion, by changing what consumers think or feel about the brand sufficiently to change their behaviour. Nor does it need to strongly differentiate brands, because most are remarkably alike in their main attributes. "In the absence of potentially persuasive messages, advertising has to be highly creative to achieve impact, interest, and memorability for the brand." They illustrated how advertising works with their ATR&N model — initial Awareness and interest stimulates a Trial purchase, after which advertising shifts to Reinforcement and brand maintenance, at times Nudging positive growth at the margin. However, to be effective, they said, **most advertising has to operate over the medium-to-longer term**, cumulatively creating, developing and reinforcing memory traces for the brand, which are often subconscious.

If we share their views, then advertising's job becomes infinitely more challenging. But if we believe *The Cluetrain Manifesto*, that consumers are immune to advertising, what role — if any — is advertising really able to play?

Can Advertising Still Build Brands?

Once there was no debate. Advertising was tasked with brand building. It was the prime marketing services discipline capable of planting the brand seed in consumers' minds and growing it into commercial success. It was generally perceived as the most viable means of building share of mind and was, without doubt, extremely effective. So what happened?

"Mass marketing" as it was known has become less "mass" and far more precise. On one hand, new technology has enabled marketers to reduce wastage and adopt specific targeting of brands, services and products. On the other, it has empowered consumers with the ability to spread their time over a multitude of entertainment and information platforms and edit out marketing messages that do not interest them. As a result, "mass media" advertising has been dethroned as the prime brand-building component of the marketing plan. Many other communications channels are available. So many, in fact, that advertising agency clients are questioning the relevance and efficacy of the traditional 30-second TV commercial and double-page spread as the primary brand-building strategy.

Increasingly, marketers use advertising in a new way — as a secondary discipline — in some cases, to "top up" specifically targeted marketing programmes, or as a tactical support mechanism when broad awareness is needed. As far as advertising agencies are concerned, great advertising can still build great brands. With some justification, they can point to historical evidence — the Marlboro Cowboy, Coca-Cola teaching the world to sing, the Singapore Girl, and hundreds more.

The issue, however, is not so simple. Great strategic planning in combination with great creativity will still build great brands, but creativity need no longer be restricted to a TV commercial or a print campaign. The new dynamics of brands, consumers and communication channels, and the complexities of their intra-relationships driven by technological advances, require more thought, more information, more brain — and **a far broader application of creativity**.

Creativity in its broadest sense is fundamental, but advertising might no longer be the conduit. Certainly, it will not be the only one.

Marketers today have the choice of many different channels to communicate with consumers — and many of them are far more capable than advertising of delivering the marketer's mantra, Return On Investment. One such route, customer relationship management (CRM), has become one of the sexy marketing disciplines. It has literally gone through the roof compared with five years ago when it was known simply as direct marketing (DM). Every marketer's goal is to be able to sit every one of his customers down and sell them his product face to face, without the distraction of competing messages. Customer relationship management allows marketers to get pretty close to doing that. Technology allows them to collect information about their customers, store it in vast databases, and communicate directly one-to-one. And it fulfils every marketer's dream in that it is accountable. It is like going back to the face-to-face selling strategies of Avon and Tupperware, but with all the efficiencies afforded by today's technology.

Strategic Versus Tactical

Advertising's changing role, particularly in Asia, is epitomised by the predominance of tactical messages over strategic. On one hand, branding is the Holy Grail. On the other, it is held at arm's length in favour of a constant stream of tactical activities designed to deliver short-term goals.

Given uncertain economic times and recurring recessions, strategic brand-building programmes are increasingly giving way to tactical promotions — driven, in part at least, by consumers' inexorable demands for greater and greater value. Advertising agencies bemoan the situation, but from their clients' viewpoint advertising dollars deliver an immediate return when invested in tactical, response-driven work. **With consumer behaviour becoming less predictable, and with audiences becoming more costly to reach, long-haul brand advertising in**

mainstream media may have seen its day. While this can partly be ascribed to the industry's consistent inability to quantify the direct return on investment from advertising, it is also a direct reflection of advertising's reduced efficacy *per se* in influencing consumer behaviour.

Advertising, however, is merely the tip of the iceberg. Marketers generally, it seems, have lost sight of long-term brand-building objectives (assuming that there were any in the first place). Within client companies in Asia marketing has become unplanned, proceeding day to day, hand to mouth. And it would be unfair to blame this situation entirely on the marketing and advertising community.

If one reflects over the Asian economic environment in recent years, it could hardly be said that the region has enjoyed the stability necessary to inspire confidence and consistent investment. Consumers and brand owners alike experienced the Asian currency crises across 1997-1998 and into the early part of 1999. A relatively good year in 2000, followed by the disastrous second half of 2001, led into a rocky 2002. Under these challenging conditions, the temptation was strong for marketers to find ways of delivering short-term sales while muddling through until conditions settled and steady growth returned. This short-termism, along with their natural inclination towards a trading mentality, has understandably led many marketers into the habit of tactical, promotion-led brand support.

And advertising is the most visible manifestation of this phenomenon. Mostly we see promotions-driven, price-led press ads, and hear loud, urgent radio commercials overloaded with special offers. The marketing purists call it sacrilege. But even if advertising is no longer the linchpin of branding, and even if advertising *per se* is no longer as effective as it used to be, **why have all the other communications channels become tactical, too?**

It is not simply a recession mentality, nor a trader mentality, on the part of marketers. It also has to do with the mentality of Asian consumers. They, too, are influenced towards a trader mentality. In fact, the Asian consumer is somewhat of a paradox. Conspicuous consumption of up-market brands in Asia is high, if not higher, than anywhere else in the world. For example, the exponential growth in the consumption of the top wines of Bordeaux and Burgundy (and preferably the best vintages) is nothing short of stunning in the top restaurants of Shanghai, Singapore and Taipei. For Mercedes-Benz, Asia has long been one of their most important regions globally. The same is true for the leading watch and jewellery brands, the fashion houses, and the likes of Louis Vuitton and Mont Blanc. In every case it is the brand, its values and what they say about an individual, that is the major driving force behind their huge demand. On the other hand, if there is a chance of a lucky draw, a 10% discount or a giveaway this will often have a dramatic effect on sales of even the most up-market luxury brands.

The Asian Marketing Dilemma

By 2020 Asia will represent two-thirds of the world's population. It already has three of the four most populous countries in the world: China (1.26 billion people), India (1 billion), and Indonesia (210 million).

Marketing across Asia's culturally disparate markets

YEAR 2020 POPULATION PROJECTIONS   (000's)

COUNTRY	2005	2020	% INCREASE
China	1,310,525	1,431,886	+ 9,3
Hong Kong	7,186	7,521	+ 4.7
India	1,090,623	1,159,516	+ 6.3
Indonesia	224,483	262,902	+17.1%
Japan	127,127	121,970	-4.1%
Korea (South)	48,928	51,870	+6.0%
Malaysia	25,460	31,035	+21.9%
Philippines	83,030	102,757	+23.8%
Singapore	4,459	5,091	+14.2%
Thailand	63,573	70,870	+11.5%
TOTAL	2,985,394	3,245,418	+8.7%

SOURCE: WORLD BANK

is far more daunting than doing the same in Europe. Europe, like Asia, has different cultures, languages and borders, even traditions of distrust and conflict. But the fundamental difference is that in Europe there are six or seven very large economies — UK, France, Spain, Italy, Germany, and Benelux — with large populations of sophisticated consumers with relatively high disposable incomes. And whether they are Dutch or German, there are many similarities to leverage within the single European community.

In comparison, China and India both have massive populations with very low average incomes. For example, of the one billion or so people in India, it is estimated that around 12%, or 120 million, represent the "middle class". However, to put their value to marketers into context, their average monthly income in urban areas is just US$200. How many pairs of jeans, how many refrigerators, can that buy?

Out of Asia's vast population of over three billion people, only a fraction — perhaps as few as 300 million individuals — have significant disposable incomes to offer a worthwhile return on marketing investment for many mid- to up-market brands. And while this is still a huge market, it is worth noting that there are 2.7 billion individuals that will not be of interest to those marketers — a number around 10 times larger than the entire population of the United States of America.

Meanwhile, countries like Vietnam with 70 million people do not even get onto the third division level of Asian

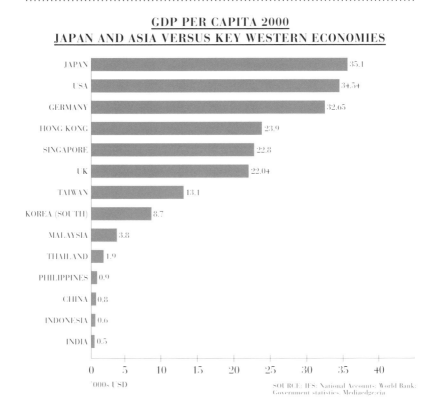

GDP PER CAPITA 2000
JAPAN AND ASIA VERSUS KEY WESTERN ECONOMIES

JAPAN	35.1
USA	34.54
GERMANY	32.65
HONG KONG	23.9
SINGAPORE	22.8
UK	22.04
TAIWAN	13.1
KOREA (SOUTH)	8.7
MALAYSIA	3.8
THAILAND	1.9
PHILIPPINES	0.9
CHINA	0.8
INDONESIA	0.6
INDIA	0.5

'000s USD

SOURCE: IFS; National Accounts; World Bank; Government statistics; Mediaedge:cia

priorities, let alone onto the radar screen of many marketers. The major fast-moving consumer goods (FMCG) players like Procter & Gamble, Colgate-Palmolive and Unilever will go into these emerging markets because of the sheer numbers, but despite their huge potential the income levels and the size of these new economies are too small to warrant major marketing communications investment.

Even in China, there are probably no more than 10 cities, albeit huge ones, that marketers would seriously pursue.

....

CHART 3: TOP 10 CHINESE CITIES AND THEIR AVERAGE HOUSEHOLD INCOMES

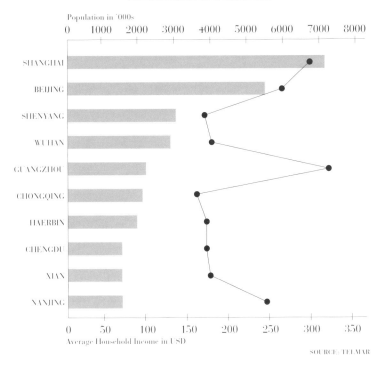

SOURCE: TELMAR

While the situation in Asia is more complex than Europe, the opportunities are much bigger and this will increasingly be the case over the coming decade. Incredibly, just over two million homes in China had a telephone in 1980. By 2000, China could boast well in excess of 144 million homes linked by fixed line telephone. As well, China today has 140 million mobile phone subscribers, outstripping even the United States in volume — yet they represent only 10% of China's total population. As other markets have shown, mobile phone penetration could conservatively be expected to increase to at least 30% in coming years. Another 280 million phones and subscriber contracts up for grabs!

Asian brands that understand Asia could steal a march on foreign-owned brands if they made the necessary (and courageous) marketing investment. If they did, they would secure the strategic opportunity of not just being successful in Asia; they could well be successful globally. The principle of "leapfrogging" is well entrenched in the Asian business psyche. Oddly enough, it is rarely applied in the brand-building context.

Infrastructure Leapfrogging: A Lesson For Asian Brands

One has only to land at the new, state-of-the-art airports of Kuala Lumpur, Hong Kong and Seoul, or the award-winning Changi airport in Singapore, to understand how far ahead many Asian markets are in relation to the infrastructures of mature Western economies. The same is true of the mass rapid transport systems of Hong Kong and Singapore.

The amazing skyline of Hong Kong, Shanghai's futuristic architecture, and the Petronas Twin Towers of Kuala

Lumpur all bear testimony to how the leading markets of Asia have leapfrogged their Western counterparts over the past decade.

Their success is due in part to the fact that many modern Asian societies are less than 40 years old. With little worthwhile infrastructure of their own in place, they were able to look at the decaying London Underground or the New York Subway, assess all the problems, and design brand new systems that were light years ahead of the century-old originals. (Meanwhile, Shanghai is building the world's first magnetic-levitation rail link that will whisk passengers from the airport to the city centre — a distance of 30 km — in just eight minutes. This US$1 billion "maglev" line, due for completion by the end of 2003, will see bullet trains travelling at 430 km/h or more. It is merely the first stage of a plan to create a mega-Shanghai, the first city in the world that will boast "maglev" links to 15 other cities within a 300-km radius, including Nanjing and Hangzhou.)

An identical opportunity exists for Asian manufacturers and traders. **They can apply the same principles of leapfrogging to develop their products into world-class brands.** By studying the flaws of decaying Western brands they can build new brand DNAs that leapfrog them, and deliver the values and benefits that both new Asian and global consumers are looking for.

Focusing Their Act

In Asia, and especially in markets such as China, when brand owners want to seize a marketing opportunity in a certain situation — and that situation is perceived as essentially simple — they too often do it themselves. For example, marketers will often go direct to media owners and buy their own media on the best terms they can get.

Shrewd horse-trading is fine in its place, but it should not lead the marketing process. The truth remains that when Asian brands take on global brands, the "financials" have to be factored out of the equation — in the early stages, at least — to enable strategic planning to have free rein. When squeezing the best deals remains the absolute priority, planning can never be objective, dispassionate and single-minded. Asian brand owners can leapfrog their foreign counterparts, but only if they focus their energies and goals. And, in some cases, relinquish control: the more complex the situation, the more they need planning from experts who deal in specific disciplines. Media coverage, for one, has become so complex, so fragmented, marketers have to go to people who are absolute experts.

The disparate and dynamic markets of Asia hold the key to future growth for many of the world's leading brands — as well as the major domestic brands of China, India and other leading markets of the region. But the billions of lost dollars invested into these markets by foreign brand owners stand as a stark warning. Market entry is at best perilous; poorly planned attempts are doomed. Complex layers of variable challenges threaten sustainable commercial success. Conventional approaches to marketing activity will more often than not fail. The key to success lies in thoroughly understanding the idiosyncrasies of doing business in each individual market.

The Future

Brands have never been under such pressure; pressure from global anti-corporation lobbyists, pressure from consumers, pressure from retailers, and even pressure from within their own companies. At the same time, and especially in the Asian context, never before has there been so much potential for brand growth and development. But the conventional brand building methodologies are just not working as effectively as before, and brand owners seem unsure where to turn for help.

Chapter 3

THE NEW CONSUMER

Don't sell me nothing.
SARL, AGE 24, JAKARTA
FROM *SECRET LIVES*™

Somebody once said, "You're a consumer. Get out there and consume." If only, if only… Today's consumers are better educated, more confident and harder to influence than ever before. They know how advertising works. They can decode it. They know when they are being patronised. They are simply not prepared to tolerate over-claiming; they haven't got the time.

And marketers and their advertising agencies find this scenario very difficult to accept. The implications of accepting it would be too difficult to deal with. If advertisers knew for sure that their target audiences were generally cynical about the concept of advertising, that they did not watch TV the way we believe they watch it, and that the majority of consumers — especially the younger ones — actively try to avoid commercial messages, it would make conventional advertising unattractive.

Naomi Klein provides an insight into the reality of consumers who have grown up with advertising: "Study after study showed that baby boomers, blind to the alluring images of advertising and deaf to the empty promises of celebrity spokespersons, were breaking their lifelong brand loyalties and choosing to feed their families with private-label brands from the supermarket, claiming heretically that they couldn't tell the difference."

Diminishing Trust

In the US, advertising agency DDB confirmed the fall in brand loyalty. In 1975, 86% of consumers aged 60-69 said they remained loyal to well known brands. By 2000, the proportion had dropped to 59%. The number of 20-29-year-olds loyal to brands fell from 66% to 59% in the same period.

In the UK, The Future Laboratory reported that brand perceptions have also declined. A recent survey by the Industrial Society in the UK gave Nike the lowest trust rating bar one.

Brands — and the companies that produce them — received a no-confidence vote in a poll by *Business Week* magazine. In 2001, two thirds of respondents agreed that "having large profits was more important to big business than developing safe, reliable, quality products for consumers". Only a quarter of those surveyed thought business was "pretty good" at being honest in its dealings with consumers. Brands were blamed for "squeezing out local business" and "reducing local variety and culture". The percentage of consumers who believed that "what is good for business is good for most Americans" declined from 71% in 1996 to 47% last year.

UK consumers displayed similar sentiments in research for the Future Foundation's nVision service. The number who agreed that most companies were fair to consumers declined from 58% in 1980 to 36% in July 2002. Three quarters of those polled believed that large multinational companies either had "too much power and should be stopped now" or that they "need to be policed and controlled more than they are at present".

Is Anybody Watching?

The sheer power and authority that commercial television held even up to a few years ago has diminished in its conventional sense.

As Ken Sacharin points out in *Attention!*, "Everywhere we look today, the power of marketing communications is eroding from lack of attention. According to one estimate, only a third of all ad campaigns have a significant impact on sales. Fewer than 25% have any long term effect."

Ad recall has dramatically declined. Sacharin quotes data that suggests in 1965, 34% of adult viewers could name one or more brands advertised in the TV programme they had just watched. By 1990, that figure had slumped to 8%.

Attention has diminished for four main reasons.

There are now so many choices available — video, VCD, DVDs, and computer games — that consumers are no longer dependent on "live" TV programming as their primary source of entertainment. As well, a massive proliferation of TV channels along with PDAs, mobile phones and the Internet all vie for their time.

Secondly, consumers are becoming "time poor". They have so little free time, and so many better things to do than be passive receivers of commercial messages. They live compressed lives. The Future Laboratory tells us that in America, from 1965 to 1995, the average news sound bite imploded from 42 seconds to just eight. In 1979 the average length of a *Time* cover story was nearly 4,500 words; today, the same story and the ideas it contains must be communicated in 2,800.

Thirdly, a growing majority of viewers are of an age that grew up with commercial television. They are so tuned into advertising codes that they are at best disbelieving, and at worst, simply don't care. In fact, a Medialab *SENSOR* survey carried out in 2001 among 8,000 respondents in Europe and the USA found that on average 45% of viewers claimed to actively avoid TV advertising. The other main media fared little better. More of this later.

The fourth reason is the generally poor and falling quality of programming. Extremely good programmes are still being made, but not enough. Content has to become more attractive to increasingly demanding viewers. Good quality content is usually very expensive. The challenge is how to fund it from revenues that are constantly being eroded by the fragmentation of viewership due to the vast increase in other channel options. Television companies know that while advertising remains a critical source of revenue, commercial breaks often trigger widespread zapping. If a viewer happens across a more attractive programme, he is lost to a competitor. **So fragmented have audiences become that rarely does any single programme command more than 20% of the available audience.** And ironically, when television does build up massive audiences through coverage of tragic events like September 11, advertisers do not want their brands associated with such stories. Perhaps the only consistent exceptions are major sporting events such as the Super Bowl.

Quantitatively, consumers are spoilt for choice. In Western economies, freed of terrestrial TV and radio controlled by governments, they are able to watch sometimes hundreds of different cable and satellite channels.

Yesterday's vast audiences have become individual moving targets. In some respects, satellite TV is more like radio than traditional TV — a very low coverage, high frequency medium. And while there are still people who are quite happy sitting in front of the TV, and who don't channel surf, an increasing amount of research shows what audiences really do in commercial breaks. For years they have gone to the bathroom, made tea or raided the fridge. Today we can add more distractions: surfing the Net, texting a friend, a quick burst on the Xbox or sending a picture to relatives from the mobile phone, to mention just a few.

More than ever before, marketers have to grapple with relevance and connectivity. If they have the right message, in the right environment, targeted to the right audience, and it is relevant to that audience, it will work — in any medium, be it TV, print, on the Internet or through customer relationship management. But if they have the wrong message, in the wrong medium, at the wrong time, or exposed to the wrong audience, it won't really matter how much money they spend.

And, in the context of the new consumer, marketers and advertising agencies now have to grapple with what constitutes a "message". It is not simply a message couched in the traditional form of advertising. It might be an ambient message, like the appearance of Evian mineral water hanging from the ceilings of Singapore's pedestrian underpasses, demonstrating the benefits of the new packaging to young adults on their way to clubs and pubs. It might be the myriad brands that have agreed product placement deals with the producers of the latest James Bond movie or *Matrix II*.

Nor can clients and advertising creatives cling to the belief that the "meaning" they put into their messages will be the one that the consumer takes out. Australia's leading social researcher Hugh Mackay long ago debunked the "Injection Myth". Advertising, he argued, does not work like a hypodermic needle. "We cling to the idea that messages are powerful and audiences are passive. It's not what our message does *to* the audience, but what the audience does *with* our message, that determines our success."

Whither The Family?

Marketers now operate in a far more socially and sexually diverse landscape, especially in Europe. The impact on brands and how they are promoted is profound. According to The Future Laboratory, such diversity means there can no longer be "ideal" family arrangements in advertising executions. "This is a generation that will demand inclusivity... Advertisers will be penalised for non-representation, or for targeting one family type over another." The brands that are more likely to succeed in an increasingly single and fragmented society will be those that "encourage and allow relationships with this new type of consumer".

While nuclear families are still key, says The Future Laboratory, they are getting smaller and richer. Couples are marrying later at 28. Today, 9.7% of all European children live in single parent households, a number that has tripled over the past two decades. The most dramatic change occurred in the UK where one in five children lives in a single parent household, up from 6.4% in 1983. And by 2005, less than half the population of the UK will be married.

New types of families emerging to challenge marketers include step-parent households, double-income-lone-kid households, single-income-now-divorced households, high-earning alpha mother-with-serial-partner households, negotiated friends-style households, and same-sex households (the latter likely to increase as a result of EU-wide legalisation).

The New Asian Consumer

People above the age of 40 remember a vastly different Asia. Older Asian consumers want a Mercedes-Benz, a Mont Blanc in their top pocket and a Rolex. They will only spend when the economy is successful. When there is a downturn they will stop spending immediately. They will wait and see. They have a very real fear of going back to the old days.

Younger Asians have only experienced a more stable, sophisticated and economically vibrant world. They have an entirely different value set. This new Asian consumer sees a far bigger picture than their elders do. They know there are peaks and troughs in the economy. They drive a BMW, they won't wear a Rolex, and they prefer vodka or wine to cognac. They want to be seen as different from the Old Guard. They want to be their own people. They want their own sense of identity. They want to be accepted for who they are, not what they are told they should be. Nor will they accept the fear that their parents try to push onto them from a past that they have never experienced.

The new Asian consumer is heavily influenced by American culture through the media. For one thing, some Asian markets are too small to sustain their own culture. Moreover, it is the individualism of American culture that young Asians find so appealing. Arguably, the new Asian consumer is far more open-minded, more individualistic. Their media habits are different, too. Text messaging has taken on a life of its own. Surfing the Net, they spend very little time watching TV. When they do, it will tend to be appointment television.

So how do marketers reach the Asian under-24s — described by the Economist Intelligence Unit as having **the highest per-capita spending power in the world** compared to their peers in other markets?

Singapore-based Red Card, one of the new breed of marketing companies springing up all over the world, conducted a radical research study branded *Secret Lives*™. It demolished sacred myths and heralded the advent of Fourth Wave Marketing. Its conclusions provided no comfort for conventional marketing wisdom. Word-of-mouth and inadvertent brand contacts emerged as the most powerful brand tools. "Everything is interconnected, nothing is extraneous, information is currency," it reported. "Media is no longer a mono-dimensional experience, it is now an impossibly complex concept, it is infinite… Advertising is no longer working: cynicism is rampant, ad-avoidance is rife... Entertainment (by brand messages) is a social obligation; brands are only diversions, marketing must be a distraction... Voyeurism is out, immersion is in..."

The proprietary study employed alternative research techniques to probe the secret lives of these most elusive, culturally discerning and difficult-to-target young Asians. Focus groups were out. ("I love doing those discussion group things," said a 19-year-old Singaporean. "You get to tell them which ads to make.") Instead, the under-24s were "stalked" by observational techniques night and day for eight days. "Buddy" teams were recruited, one as subject, one as recorder, in four Asian trendsetter cities — Jakarta, Kuala Lumpur, Manila and Singapore.

Seven areas of inquest centred primarily on media consumption and new media opportunities. **Media habits** were exhaustively recorded — which buttons were wearing down on the TV remote control, and how many programmes were being watched simultaneously? How did **technology** impact their lives, and how were their technology purchase decisions influenced? **Hang time** was logged, including distractions: how bored were they, and what did they talk about at burger bars? A **clothing audit** saw wardrobes emptied and logged; what was worn with what, how was individuality expressed in a collective culture? The **days of the week** were differentiated, revealing rituals, patterns, and geographical footprints. Their **daily patterns** recorded what they did, ate, and smoked, where they went and whether they planned ahead or improvised. Their **fast (and slow) food consumption** was mapped from idea, to craving, the journey to the outlet and the influences along the way;

could soft drink brand choices be influenced between the point of decision and the point of purchase?

_____*Secret Lives*™ posed the question: **Why are the world's lowest consumers of media some of the best-informed people on the planet?**

Asian youth consumes less and less conventional media. Newspapers are studiously avoided; magazines are too expensive; they are more likely to read tray-liners in fast food outlets. Radio has been replaced by MP3. TV grazing is limited to four shows a week on Channel V. Everything in their lives is orchestrated, down to the type of batteries they run their Walkmans on. Everything is carefully considered after detailed consultation with friends and peers. Their rampant thirst for knowledge is driven by a relentless hunt for peer-driven information, fed through invisible channels. This points to a future for brand communications that is built "media-up", rather than "creative-down". The age of the creative big idea seems to have come to an end. Successful brands succeed despite their advertising.

The under-24s are a generation of compulsive ad-avoiders: "Their sophisticated ability to detect and then avoid brand marketing seems to have been genetically wired into their systems." They remain almost totally oblivious to incoming marketing messages. They have developed a "marketing blind spot": few TV ads are witnessed, and when they are, more often than not they are zoned out. On-line advertising is screened out. Outdoor media is routinely missed. "Institutionalised cynicism" pervades everything: they know brands are playing to a weakness, they suspect the hidden agendas of marketers, yet they are the most voracious brand advocates — not only in terms of brand consumption, but the way they use brands as personal co-ordinates. "Brands seem to play an almost metaphysical role. These young consumers navigate the world of peer group and friendship by means of and through brands."

Some lessons for marketers:

1. Well-branded messages are the least effective because who wants to live a 'sponsored life'?
2. Creative advertising is the most despised because it "nearly works".
3. Sales messages elicit the opposite effect. The ones to avoid can be identified as the ones who are trying to reach you.
4. The more you shout, the more they ignore you. They associate repeat viewings with parrot-like learning in an unenlightened school.
5. Unbranded content works better than branded.
6. "Accidental brand contact" is welcomed because it reveals more about the brand, and thus says more about "me".
7. Naked honesty works.
8. Life is not a rehearsal so why should all communication look and feel routine?

Loud and brash is not the way to go, immersive entertainment is. Asian youth is perpetually bored, spending idle hours outside congested family homes, hanging out in burger bars, teashops, and ubiquitous US-style malls. Diversions are everything. Brands, they contend, have a duty to entertain them. A brand's entertainment value will be judged by its ability to surprise, constantly, with little or no repetition. A brand message should demonstrate "insider" knowledge and feel like it came from one of their own tribe. Brand messages must lead somewhere; diversion value comes from prolonged engagement and prolonged distraction. Their assessment of brand messages is black and white: "That's cool," or "That's not."

When marketers get it right and get under their radar, they can unleash a tidal storm of interconnectivity. Entertainment confers viral status on brand messages. "New media", encompassing guerilla marketing, viral marketing, buzz, street and womb marketing, work as catalysts to influence youth. As part of an idea currency, passed on and exchanged incessantly, they can deflect purchasing intentions, change the geographical footprint of a subject's movement through a retail environment, alter seemingly repetitive purchasing behaviour, increase frequency of purchase, and positively influence consideration sets across many different categories.

Secret Lives™ concluded that inadvertent brand contact is perhaps the only truly effective brand communications tool available today. Accidental, incidental, and apparently unpredictable, it is built on seemingly unconnected chance encounters, interwoven and interconnected like "brand hyperlinks", revealing the brand slowly, intelligently, flirtatiously, making the consumer do the work, not pouring it all out in one execution. The consumer must be placed in the action, not simply in front of the action. By seeding ideas, brands can intrigue young consumers and leave them to join the dots themselves.

Now, about that TV commercial…

"Irritation Value"

Once, a certain global advertising agency's credo waxed lyrical about the "irritation value" of TV commercials. In order to sell successfully, the agency told its clients, commercials should be repetitive and irritating so that they drilled themselves into the consumer's mind. The more irritating they were, the more consumers would remember them. Irritation was thus a virtuous goal. Today, it spells disaster.

Certain forms of communication are becoming incredibly irritating, to the point where they become negative for the brand and the advertiser. What marketers should be asking themselves about their advertising is not just "Will it be effective?" but "Will it become an irritation?" Understanding *how* consumers will receive a message is critical for success. Radio audiences habitually listen to the same drivetimes and don't want to hear the same commercial repeated three or four times in the half hour it takes to get to work. Likewise, satellite TV channels often screen endless repeats of the same commercials. If advertisers do not know how to use the media, it is coming to a point where their audiences will simply tune them out — or turn them off.

Only occasionally do we see a medium used powerfully that takes into account the way its audience receives the content. When Famous Grouse Scotch Whisky sponsored the broadcast of the 1999 Rugby World Cup, aired in Asia on Star Sports, the client and ad agency recognised that hardcore rugby fans would be likely to watch many of the games from start to finish. Clearly, the relatively small yet valuable audience would be exposed to a considerable number of commercial breaks with the pre-, mid- and post-match commentaries. Rather than irritate them with endless repeats of the same commercial, they produced over 20 amusing vignettes that were constantly changed to reflect the status of any given game and the teams playing. Sadly however, for that one strong example there are hundreds of appalling cases where a medium has been poorly used and opportunities have been lost. Frankly, it can usually be put down to laziness. Either the client is not listening to the advice he is being given, or he is not being given any advice at all. Which is simply not acceptable.

The Grey Area

Most large mature economies like the US, Europe and Japan have dramatically aging populations, especially in comparison to many Asian markets. As time progresses and people live longer, fewer younger people will be working to support more older people. The mature economies have yet to register the full effects of underplanning for retirement costs. The pressure that will put, directly and indirectly, on the working population has yet to be witnessed.

Japan is the world's most rapidly aging society. Its birthrate is declining — currently at 1.33 per hundred — and its workforce shrinking. Japanese seem to live longer than other nationalities. Men can expect to live up to 78, women up to 85. (By 2050, those figures will climb to 81 and 89 respectively.) At present 17.4% of the Japanese population is above 65. By 2015, that ratio will rise to one in four, the world's highest. Japan is already taking action to stave off the burden on its pension system. The government will raise the minimum retirement age, and encourage retirees to return to the workforce. The carrot will be a new pension deferment system, which will in effect earn them larger pensions when they do finally stop work. Meanwhile, the Health Ministry has earmarked one trillion yen (over US$8 billion) to make having children more attractive by boosting child support facilities and programmes. Only 1.17 million babies were born in 2001, Japan's lowest number, and far from the peak of two million births in the 1970s. An average rate of 2.1 births per woman over her lifetime is required for the Japanese population to replace itself. But all evidence points to the fact that within 30 years Japan's total population will have reduced by as much as 10 million. Not surprisingly, increasing the birth rate has become a national priority.

Asia, on the other hand, has a comparatively much younger population. And projecting forward 10 or 15 years, Asia will still have larger numbers of people working, still generating wealth. Typically, when economists and marketers look at Asia, its demographics are attractive — apparently without the time bomb the older economies have. However, a closer look at the data reveals that even the younger societies of Asia will experience their own version of the aging demographic time bomb. Projections for China, for example, show that the population over 65 years of age is set to increase by 168% — from around 98 million individuals in 2005 (representing around 7.5% of the population) to a massive 262 million (representing 17.5% of the total population) by 2030. To put this into context, this number of individuals would on their own represent the fourth largest country in the world based on today's populations. Other Asian markets with similar issues ahead are Malaysia, Singapore, and most notably Hong Kong, which is expected to have nearly 30% of its population over 65 years by 2030 — a percentage even higher than Japan.

....

COMPARISON OF AGING DEMOGRAPHICS IN ASIA AND JAPAN

COUNTRY	Population over 65yrs ('000s)		Population over 65yrs ('000s)		
	2005 ('000s)	% OF TOTAL POPULATION	2030 ('000s)	+/-%	+/-% OF TOTAL POPULATION
Japan	21,517	17.0%	33,211	+54.3%	+28.1%
China	97,850	7.5%	262,002	+168.0%	+17.5%
Hong Kong	834	11.6%	2,221	+166.0%	+29.9%
India	56,100	5.1%	113,900	+103.0%	+10.3%
Indonesia	11,506	5.1%	27,371	+138.0%	+9.6%
Korea (South)	3,995	8.1%	10,116	+158.0%	+19.1%
Malaysia	1,182	4.6%	3,529	+199.0%	+10.3%
Singapore	355	8.0%	1,156	+226.0%	+21.8%
Thailand	3,948	6.2%	9,702	+146.0%	+13.0%

SOURCE: CHINA STATISTICAL YEAR BOOK 1999; ACNIELSEN HK; STATISTICAL OUTLINE OF INDIA 2000-2001; WORLD BANK; NATIONAL CENSUS JAPAN 2000; KOREAN NATIONAL STATISTICS OFFICE 1995; POPULATION AND HOUSING CENSUS OF MALAYSIA 2000; YEAR BOOK OF STATISTICS 2000; AUSTRALIAN BUREAU OF STATISTICS 1999

....

The changes in consumer attitudes and behaviours, and their relationships with media channels and the commercial messages being aimed at them, have far-reaching implications. No longer will consumers unquestioningly accept what they see, hear or read — assuming, of course, that they paid any attention to it in the first place. In many cases, as we have seen, these commercial messages have become an extreme irritant. And this presents fundamental challenges to brand owners and their marketing advisors.

Chapter 4. A NEW APPROACH O CHANNELS

You can't sell a man who isn't listening.
BILL BERNBACH

The words of the great Bill Bernbach of Doyle Dane Bernbach are more prophetic now than when he spoke them 40 years ago.

How can marketers fully comprehend the immense challenges that they face in today's communications world? Firstly, by undertaking a reasonably thorough and open-minded review of the massive numbers of communications channels and methods available. And secondly, through considering how the strategic planning of these myriad options, alternatives and combinations can best be tackled.

To begin, let us classify communications channels as **any means, media or discipline of communicating with or influencing a consumer**. Be it conventional paid-for advertising, public relations, sponsorship, or customer relationship management. Be it those channels managed through methods such as buzz marketing or episodic marketing. Be it a television commercial, a full page press ad, a sporting event, a sign on a toilet door, or a global customer loyalty programme.

Every marketing discipline, every marketing method, and every communication channel, is a legitimate option. And every possible combination of the choices available today is equally legitimate.

In this "solutions-neutral" environment, a different approach is required. Let us describe this function as communications channel planning (CCP).

A communications channel planner, after going through due process, might propose a combination of customer relationship management with public relations and some conventional advertising (perhaps used in an unconventional way) based on an episodic marketing approach.

Proliferation Of Communication Channels

There are now so many more channels of communication, and so many more opportunities to both look for and receive information, that consumers are not spending nearly as much time as they were with the conventional channels. And when they are, they are not consuming them in the old ways — either in terms of their attention or their attitudes to what they are seeing, hearing or reading.

As we have seen, the new channels, and the nature of media, are directly affecting consumer behaviour. Some brand new media channels offer fresh possibilities that were not available as recently as a year ago.

Massive audience fragmentation means that consumers are now more expensive and challenging to reach. But there is no question that they can be effectively reached in media environments where they are passionate about everything to do with those environments. The corollary is that the brand must not offend, intrude, waste time or distract — many of the criticisms that brands have engendered over the years. Today's new consumers will not tolerate them. In other words, brand messages have to be respectful and relevant.

In this new era of consumer power, audience fragmentation, proliferating communications channels and diversity of brands, it is clear that marketing overall needs a fresh approach. Study after study tells us that marketing in general, and advertising in particular, are becoming less and less effective. And we have to question why this is the case.

We have established, as many before us have done, that consumers define brands and that consumers therefore decide whether a brand will be a commercial success or an expensive failure. **It is therefore entirely logical to approach every single aspect of the marketing of any given brand from the consumer's point of view.**

Until as recently as five years ago, the general approach to marketing practices was effectively driven by convention. What has worked in the past? (Nearly always TV advertising.) And what is needed to support this? (Maybe some print advertising, some trade activity, some direct mail to core potential consumers, and some PR if the brand were "newsy" enough.)

At that time there were relatively few choices and marketers could consider every available option and combination of options, dismissing those that were not felt to be right and coming to a final broad plan to achieve the desired objectives. And often this approach was successful. The conventional wisdom was: If it ain't broke, don't fix it!

Today, marketers must face the fact that it is well and truly broken, and it does need fixing. Not just a superficial patch-up, but a fundamental redesign and reconstruction.

To put the new realities of marketing options into context, it would be helpful to explore the process of choices and decisions that marketers face in today's brave new world.

Today's Approach To Channels

While marketers have more strategic options than ever before, too often they tread the same well-worn paths. Put it down to habit, the fear factor, lack of knowledge, flawed advice, or the fact that the advertising industry has remained unchanged for decades, today's options remain largely underutilised. Yet a growing voice, especially among the more sophisticated marketers, is demanding fundamental change in the way their agencies work and think.

Communications plans are usually concocted in an arbitrary way. The ad agency might say, "Here is the television commercial", which in effect means that much of the communications and media planning has already been pre-empted. Or it might be the marketer saying, "What I think we need is sales promotion and some TV..." Again, game, set, match.

Rarely will communications channel planning be conducted in an objective, solutions-neutral way with clearly defined, measurable objectives and built around a powerful process. Rather, it happens in a very tactical, executionally-led way and is often based on historical precedent.

What needs to be done? Everything has to be turned on its head. Everything has to be approached strategically with the consumer at the heart of all thought. And nothing should be done until the whole plan has been worked out. Everything should be put in the right place, at the right time, so each has a layered, multiplier effect on the other. And it should be made concretely measurable over time.

On the following pages we will develop a simple matrix built around the brand issue or task that has to be addressed. It is far from exhaustive, but it is helpful in that it progressively explores the interlinked options, marketing disciplines, processes and communication channels available to marketers today and demonstrates the literally millions of permutations in terms of achieving a solution. It is not intended as a process that should be applied to marketing problems, but simply a way of demonstrating the magnitude and complexity of marketing today.

1. The starting point is often an assumed marketing issue based on either a **brand issue or task**.

**Brand
Issue/task**

2. The matrix sets out some of the typical issues and tasks that marketers believe their brands face. Moving clockwise from the top:

The marketer may perceive that he needs to **generate more loyalty** for his brand if, for example, the brand is losing market share to a competitor. His existing customer base may need shoring up to ensure repeat sales.

He may perceive the need to run a **tactical promotion** to achieve a specific sales or market share objective.

Relaunching or repositioning of the brand may drive the agenda. Perhaps the brand has lost its relevance or requires updating.

Perhaps a competitor has launched a new brand, and thus the issue may be caused by a **competitive reaction**.

Perhaps the marketing objective is as straightforward as **sales maintenance**, or is it time to **launch a new product**?

In some cases, the cells in the diagram may be interlinked. One cell may represent the task or issue, or it could comprise two or more cells in combination.

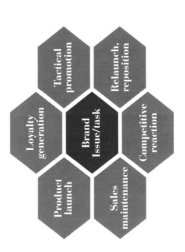

3. Next, the marketer will consider some of the broad strategic options that can be employed to solve the problem:

- Customer relationship management
- A customer service programme
- Distribution chain activities
- Staff incentives
- A sales training programme
- A corporate identity programme
- Episodic marketing
- Buzz marketing
- Public relations
- Sales promotion
- On-line activity
- Advertising

(On this menu, note that advertising is only *one* of the marketer's options).

4. Once broad strategic options have been considered and a short list drawn up, the marketer will often then evaluate some of the **specific communication channels and tactics**, including:

Brand contact at point of sale. Perhaps the marketer believes the solution lies with getting closer to the consumer at the point of purchase?

Brand contact at point of service. Or should the brand be looking to develop activities that put it closer to the consumer at the point of service?

Brand contact in retail outlets. Possibly the marketer is looking to garner support from the trade — by spending his marketing budget with retailers and building partnership solutions with his most important sales influencers?

Permission marketing. Does the nature of the brand dictate that permission marketing is a valid approach to brand-consumer connectivity?

3G WAP. Does new technology present an option for the marketer to meet the needs of the brand in relation to the behaviour of the consumer?

Celebrity endorsement. Will the brand benefit from an appropriate celebrity talking about the virtues of the product or service?

Packaging. Is it still working or does it need redesigning?

Advertorials. Will the connection between the media vehicle and the brand provided by advertorials aid in achieving the objectives, or will the sophisticated reader take one look at the "Advertising Promotion" header and turn the page?

Sampling. How can the marketer get the product into the

Spas

Carparks

Permission marketing

3G WAP

Celebrity endorsement

Environmental

Bars, clubs

Retail outlets

Distribution

Staff incentives

Sales training

Packaging

Point of service contact

Customer service

Tactical promotion

Relaunch, reposition

Corporate identity

Advertorial

POS

CRM

Loyalty generation

Brand issue/task

Competitive reaction

Episodic marketing

Sampling

Print

Advertising

Product launch

Sales maintenance

Buzz marketing

Product placement

Kiosks

Outdoor

On-line

Sales promotion

PR

Sponsorship

Co-branding

Cinema

Radio

TV

Exhibitions

Events

Sports marketing

Airports

Inflight

Digital television

Guerilla tactics

Sky media

Phone cards

hands of the consumer so that they can judge by experiencing it whether this is a product they wish to purchase?

Product placement. What would be the benefits of having the product seen in movies or on TV, being handled by popular personalities? And can the marketer control the environment?

On-line. What role can the Net play in building relationships with consumers?

Sponsorship. Will the association of the brand with a sporting, musical or charity event have a positive impact on the consumer?

Event marketing. Is there an opportunity to create a specially tailored event to promote the brand in an interesting and relevant manner?

Exhibitions. Should the marketer consider participation in exhibitions?

Public relations. What would be the value of a professionally orchestrated PR campaign, with the benefits that it would be seen as coming from the "objective" media rather than being self promotion?

Television advertising. Is there a role for the conventional brand-building route?

Radio advertising. Does radio offer a cost-efficient way of promoting the brand, especially if it has a time-of-day sensitivity?

Outdoor advertising. Can Out Of Home exposure, perhaps in airports or on a highly targeted basis, play an effective role in the communications plan?

Print advertising. Does the product or service require longer copy to explain more about the detail of the brand or a specific offer around the brand?

Clearly, there are many more issues or tasks that a marketer might face, and many more strategic and tactical options available. These cells represent just some of them. Other valid channels and methodologies are **phone cards, sky media, guerilla tactics, digital television, inflight media, airports, cinema, kiosks, bars and clubs, and spas**, to name but a few.

The purpose of this matrix is to do no more than demonstrate the complexities faced by marketers when they are considering how to play the three-dimensional chess game of connecting their brands to the right consumers, at the right time, through the most appropriate channels and contact points. When you include the hundreds of different print titles, the vast array of TV and radio stations, the millions of web sites and so on, it becomes apparent that today's marketer is faced with an infinitely more challenging world than he was five years ago. In the second part of this book we will examine methodologies and explore strategies that can manage this highly complex world.

The reality is plain. There are infinite permutations of brand issues or tasks, multiplied by countless options for the strategic use of marketing disciplines and the ever-increasing range of processes and methodologies, cubed by thousands of available media channels.

Given this reality it is not possible to take a bottom-up approach to marketing that starts with a TV commercial and have any realistic expectation of success.

With the millions of possible permutations of

solutions, a new marketing communications approach is mandatory. One that is born out of insight into consumer behaviours and attitudes, the brand's relationship with the consumer, and a clear understanding of the strategic and tactical values, individually and collectively, of the channels and consumer connection points.

In the next chapters we will explore the nature of the marketing disciplines and processes, and the media channels, in more detail. Each of these could easily represent a book in its own right. As such, we will confine our analysis to the key strategic points of each, and how they can work both independently and in combination — in other words, **their inter- and intra-relativity**.

Chapter 5. A DIVERSITY OF DISCIPLINES

The day when the brand was seen as an authority figure is over. We are entering a new world, with new media — an interactive age that asks the brand to come down off the mountain and enter into a conversation. The only way we can animate this kind of brand is to be clear what its core values are, hold fast to those and let everything else enter the flux.
DAN WIEDEN

By putting himself into the shoes of the consumer, the communications channel planner will combine different disciplines and media channels to build a marketing communications plan from the top down. As Harper Lee observed, "You only really get to know a man when you get in his shoes and walk around a bit."

For communications channel planning to have the best chance of success, three critical conditions must be met: a truly willing marketer, an appropriately skilled and resourced communications channel planner, and a rigorous and flexible process. And as you will see, communications channel planning — and then the implementation of those plans — brings strategic discipline to each facet of marketing communications, and the way each slots together within the master communications plan.

In this chapter, each marketing discipline will be explored *briefly* from the channel planner's perspective. It is a demonstration of some of the elements in a planner's armoury and how these might work together. It is not intended to be an exhaustive examination of each discipline's strengths.

THE DISCIPLINES
Advertising

Jeremy Bullmore offers a typically erudite definition of advertising: "Any paid-for communication intended to inform and/or influence one or more people."

And while this is a perfectly valid definition, with a little thought one can start to visualise the hundreds of different ways that advertising could manifest itself. Not surprisingly, it is the subject of countless books in its own right. Because advertising will be explored in greater depth in later chapters, for now we will examine its role in marketing communications today and its relationship with other disciplines.

Despite a growing weight of opinion that questions its efficacy, advertising has always been seen as the most effective way of persuading the consumer to behave in a different way. The risk is that consumers are becoming immune to what more and more of them perceive as manipulation. Nevertheless, advertising remains a massive global industry with an estimated annual turnover in excess of US$300 billion.

Historically, advertising always led the marketing communications process to the consumer. But given the explosion of consumer choices and the influence of media channels on consumer behaviour, it is understandable why its conventional role is being challenged. While some forms of advertising — TV, for example — can still create a significant amount of noise about a brand, the value of that noise needs to be very carefully considered in today's communications context. As Ken Sacharin articulates: "Most conventional media advertising works through 'borrowed attention'. The brand pays to borrow the attention of the audience to a programme or editorial. Borrowing attention is inherently interruptive and often intrusive."

Of course advertising will often continue to play a role, but it should be considered along with all the available disciplines in the solutions-neutral context of communications channel planning and not necessarily as the lead for all marketing communications activity. **Long gone are the days when the 30-second TV commercial was the *de facto* brand and marketing strategy.**

Because there are so many different forms of advertising and so many different media channels, the next chapter will explore the different applications of TV, press, magazines, ambient, radio, cinema and out of home (OOH) media within the context of communications channel planning.

Direct Marketing (DM) and Customer Relationship Management (CRM)

What was referred to somewhat unkindly as the junk mail industry has enjoyed a fair degree of success by reinventing itself. Unsexy, unfashionable DM has become CRM, customer relationship management. In some senses the sector has managed to achieve the Holy Grail, moving upstream to become a "strategic partner" — and, as such, a far more attractive proposition for brand owners.

While this shift has demanded considerable investment, it edges the business concept away from being an executional one — a direct mailing piece — into a more strategic role: managing the ongoing interface with a brand's customers.

Usually brand owners allocate a separate budget for their specialist CRM consultancy. Some, most often in service sectors, have needs such that they have developed their own highly sophisticated in-house CRM departments.

Like advertising, CRM is a massive subject and is exerting a growing influence over brand behaviour. One only has to look at marketers like Dell Computers to see how deeply the discipline is interwoven into their business models. One of Dell's key differentiators is that it does not distribute through a retail network, but purely through direct-to-consumer sales. By cutting out the middleman and passing the retail margins directly to consumers, they are able to create the perception of better value. And of course, every customer's details are captured for future marketing opportunities. Amazon.com provides a useful example of CRM working at its best. When a customer logs on to the site, he is provided with a list of suggested titles based on his previous interests and purchases. The service goes even further by stating the secondhand value of all the books he has purchased to date.

Marketers, working with channel planners, can find strategic ways of inter-relating databases from some of the more conventional media channels with their own databases. For example, many international newsweeklies and fashion magazines have substantial databases of subscribers. *Elle* magazine's core readers are extremely loyal and very connected to that magazine. For the appropriate brands, fusing the magazine's database with their own presents a powerful way of connecting with additional valuable consumers as well as enhancing commercial messages in *Elle*.

Developments in digital and interactive television also present opportunities to use conventional media routes to capture data on individuals that will allow brand interfaces. As with all communications though, caution is necessary. The often negative reaction by consumers to unsolicited mail, whether it be in hard form or electronic, is well known.

Sponsorship

Sponsorship marketing is becoming increasingly ubiquitous — from sports, the arts and television programmes, to charities and education. Historically, sponsorships have offered opportunities to step away from the clutter and own a prestigious event, be it a motor race, a concert or an art exhibition. The desired response from consumers is one of "gratitude" or goodwill.

The issue for the communications channel planner is simple: a sponsorship has to be strategically designed within the communications plan, rather than going off at a tangent because it happens to suit some individual in the marketer's organisation who likes golf or music. Such sponsorships might enhance corporate entertainment opportunities, but do they really connect with consumers?

Marketers often believe the sponsorship cost itself is where the matter ends. As a rule of thumb they need to spend at least as much again on promoting the sponsorship beyond its immediate environment if they really want to leverage its full value for the brand.

One of the key factors behind the dramatic growth in sponsorship globally is the continuous objective of brand owners trying to avoid clutter. Somewhat ironically, sponsorship clutter has itself become a major problem for the communications industry.

Sales Promotions

Like other disciplines, sales promotions have to be strategic and tasked to the brand's objectives. However, the definition of a sales promotion is becoming increasingly unclear. It can be part ambient, part point of sale, and in the case of FMCG products, part of supermarket media and part of trade communications and relationships. Often promotions are executed tactically and very badly. In Asia particularly there is a propensity to bastardise the brand in the process.

Once a support function to advertising, sales promotion and merchandising have now become primary disciplines, often working in tandem with brand advertising to achieve a short-term sales objective to encourage both the trade and the consumer to stock up. As long ago as 1987, merchandising and sales promotion accounted for 65% of total marketing communications expenditure by national advertisers in the US. As a result advertising investment had been cut back to 35%, according to the American Association of Advertising Agencies.

By definition, a sales promotion is tactical. But any tactic has to be born out of a strategy. The communications channel planner will make sales promotions strategic within the context of the total communications plan, if necessary spanning a range of different disciplines and media channels to create a layering effect — supermarket media, SMS, and conventional advertising, for example.

Many marketers will admit their sales promotion

programmes are disastrous. Under pressure, they throw money at promotions ("Buy one, get one free") without really understanding what it does to their consumers, their brands and their product sales cycles. Frequently when brands have nothing new to say, sales promotions end up giving something away and completely distracting from the value of the brand.

Event Marketing

Event marketing perfectly demonstrates how the lines between the different disciplines have blurred. Staging an event could be part of a sales promotion or connected to CRM in order to collect databases, or to encourage brand sampling. Advertising might support the event, which in turn might be linked to a sponsorship.

Holistic channel planning keeps everything strategic, inter-related and relevant. As the result of a clear insight, for example, the best connection with consumers for a new luxury car launch could be the sponsorship of a very high quality classical music event. One major event might be followed by others, in a series of episodes. That central theme would then be diffused through various other disciplines, using the database of an arts magazine and generating word of mouth.

Public Relations

In many ways, mainstream PR was the first form of viral marketing. It ideally engages the consumer through objective channels to promote for the benefit of the brand.

In the context of communications channel planning,

PR would have a defined, strategic role within the overall communications mix.

Rather than saying "we need some PR" or "we need some sales promotion" or "we need some CRM", the channel planning process will identify the best ways of connecting consumers with the brand. PR could come out of that strategic understanding as one of the best ways to connect with consumers. Clearly this is far more likely to be the case when the brand story has some newsworthiness.

If one of the strategies of the communications plan were to promote a brand or product through third-party endorsement, then PR and viral marketing would become obvious routes. For movie marketers, book publishers and car manufacturers, there is nothing stronger than third-party endorsement — strong reviews in objective newspapers and magazines.

Rather than being independently implemented, PR would become a strategic discipline within the master communications plan. It would be integrated knowing the boundaries of what the marketer is trying to achieve and the budget he has. The PR firm would be briefed right at the outset so it understood its role in the process, and how its part of the process would be managed. In that context, there is a very valuable connection to be made with media specialists. Because of their deep understanding of the qualitative and quantitative aspects of audience delivery through the various media channels, media specialists can play a helpful role in identifying media channel priorities for PR activity.

PROCESSES

Given both the speed of change within the brand, media and consumer dynamic, and the constant development of new marketing processes and methodologies, this section provides purely a snapshot of some of the opportunities available to marketers. Any of these processes can be utilised within a communications channel plan, either in isolation or in combination.

Episodic Marketing

Developed by Fusion 5 in Connecticut USA, episodic marketing is a process designed to reflect the changing dynamics of consumer behaviour. In part it addresses the fact that brands have increasingly shorter life cycles and that within those, consumer interest often drops away far too quickly following a brand launch. In the cosmetics category, for example, many perfume marketers launch two or sometimes three new fragrances every year. No sooner are they launched than their sales start declining, while the classic fragrances endure for generations. An episodic approach can deliver sustained sales for new brands by lengthening their interest to consumers.

Episodic marketing endeavours to create brand-consumer relationships that have saliency over time. It would manifest itself in a series of different episodes of marketing activity, going out over a long period of time. Each one builds on the last, creating news and "buzz" about the brand, keeping consumers interested and coming back to buy it again — rather than spending the launch or relaunch budget in one big burst. The communications channel planner might divide the budget over, say, 10 strategic episodes.

The world of movies and TV programmes provides a helpful analogy of this approach. In the past, marketers tended to work to a "blockbuster" strategy for the launch or relaunch of a brand, often spending all their budget in one or two short bursts of activity that would create deep and immediate impact, but would then taper away relatively quickly. This strategy is akin to the launch of an epic movie such as *Titanic*. The launch "noise" was immense, but dropped off quickly. However, episodic marketing is more akin to *X-Files*, a series of high quality programmes going out over a sustained period of time to keep viewers (or consumers) involved and motivated, and importantly achieving a cumulative build of interest in the brand.

Buzz Marketing

Closely related to episodic marketing, buzz marketing identifies key opinion formers and persuades them to lead the brand into the market. Sometimes this is achieved directly through recruiting individuals who are leaders in their schools, universities, clubs and discos; people who are the style leaders and opinion formers of their groups. This goes as far as some brands paying video deejays, the style leaders of youth, to wear their products or be seen drinking their products, to create a buzz about the brand.

The reason buzz marketing works is logical enough. As we saw in Red Card's *Secret Lives*™ research study, young people are very cynical about advertising, but very astute about what is the thing to be seen wearing or where is the place to be seen drinking. They are incredibly fashion conscious and open to being influenced on that, but become far less open when an advertiser tells them what they should do in a more dictatorial manner.

Given that it is as important not to be seen in the wrong places as it is to be seen in the right places, environment and message content are crucial buzz marketing factors. In Bartle Bogle Hegarty's Asian campaign for Levi's Original Engineered Jeans, pop culture icons climbed onto the world's largest copier. It combined the principles of ambient media and buzz marketing — and then unleashed viral marketing.

Buzz marketing is developing as a viable method of connecting brands to consumers in a way that is unobtrusive and impactful. Buzz is an effective way to market new movies. Once, running movie trailers on TV and buying big press ads were the conventional means of attracting cinema audiences. Recently, research confirmed that word of mouth would be highly effective, provided of course that the movie was liked. (If the movie were disappointing, then buzz or word of mouth would prove highly damaging to its success.) Movie marketers now seek opportunities to hold sneaks and previews, generating as much buzz and hype as possible among target moviegoers. As we have seen with the under-24s, peer recommendations carry more weight than any amount of mass media advertising.

Viral Marketing

If consumers' lips are the best medium of all, then viral marketing can come a close second. It is hard to control and can backfire if any element of the message is not true, is open to misinterpretation, or is patronising. Consumers are

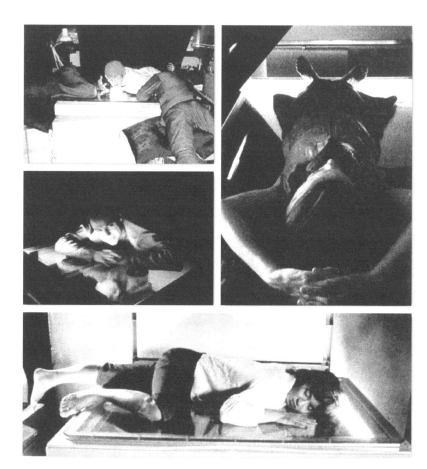

Bartle Bogle Hegarty's Asian campaign for Levi's Original Engineered Jeans combined the principles of ambient media and buzz marketing. Pop icons and consumers climbed onto the world's biggest photocopier, creating hundreds of original campaign images.

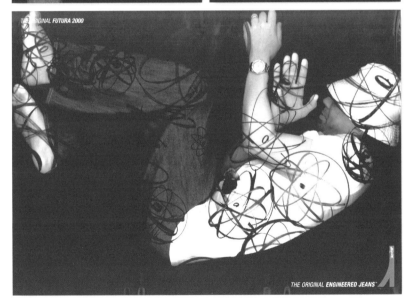

more likely to share their negative brand experiences with far greater alacrity than their positive ones.

How can viral marketing be defined? Author Malcolm Gladwell wrote: "The best way to understand the dramatic transformation of unknown books into bestsellers, or the rise of teenage smoking, or the phenomena of word of mouth or any number of the other mysterious changes that mark everyday life, is to think of them as epidemics. Ideas and products and messages and behaviours spread just like viruses do…" Ideas spread virally can become fulcrums of drastic change.

The theory of memetics foreshadowed viral marketing. Back in 1976, Richard Dawkins coined the term "meme" — a replicator that allows information to be copied and passed on **by imitation** in an evolutionary process. Self-replicating memes can be habits, skills, stories or games passed on by imitation. Some of the earliest viruses of the mind were the contents of chain letters.

Arguably, TV commercials being shared on the Net are also memes. Consumers will happily share their favourite ads, provided the commercials have something to say that is genuinely interesting. Equally, if there is something really negative about a TV commercial, they will spread that with 10 times the energy. People want to be seen to be spreading unique, "must see" messages. They certainly would not share something boring with their peers. Nothing is more irritating than being on the receiving end of a boring brand viral message.

Photo messaging is taking off across Europe, reinforcing teenagers' use of mobile technology to enhance their social activities. As the retail cost of new generation handsets comes down, photo messaging will expand the possibilities of viral marketing dramatically.

The downside is that while viral marketing has power, it is unpredictable, uncontrollable, and non-schedulable.

Other viable methodologies now include **permission marketing, guerrilla marketing** and the whole concept of **attention marketing**, of which Ken Sacharin is a leading proponent. His book *Attention!* is a valuable source of wisdom and insight.

Chapter 6. MEDIA ROUTES

To borrow a metaphor from Darwinian theory, the attention environment is becoming inhospitable to ads. To survive, new "fitter" species of ads are evolving. But the rate of advertising evolution cannot keep pace with the rate of deterioration in the attention ecology. Almost every day we find reason to be amazed by new ad forms that explore new niches. But as rapidly as the ad forms evolve, their survival is undermined by even more rapid deterioration in the attention ecosystem.
KEN SACHARIN

In the early years of the twenty-first century, we can already glimpse the future of mass media. In Ken Sacharin's words: "When the media multiply, audiences divide."

However, once we talk in terms of communications channels, our perspective widens.

The delivery of communications channel planning and the implementation of that plan will be explored in later chapters. For now, to help in understanding how channel planning works, it is necessary to first examine the realities of both traditional and new media. Throughout much of this chapter, an important research study into advertising clutter and ad avoidance will be frequently referenced. Conducted in 2001 by media specialist Mediaedge:cia, the *SENSOR* survey was undertaken among 8,000 households in Europe and the US. Its invaluable insights tell us how consumers behave in relation to commercial messages in the key media channels.

TRADITIONAL MEDIA
Television

As long ago as 1990, George Gilder predicted in *Life after Television* that the mass nature of the medium was set for dramatic change: "The medium will change from a mass-produced and mass-consumed commodity to an endless feast of niches and specialities… A new age of individualism is coming. It will bring an eruption of culture unprecedented in human history."

Powerful words, and it is this very de-massing of the medium in content and audience that is changing its value to marketers. As TV channels multiply and audiences divide, the convention that brands can only be built through TV is becoming increasingly challenged. It is fair to state that relatively few marketers or their advisors have yet grasped the nature of these changes and harnessed them for the commercial success of brands. As we saw from the *Secret Lives*™ research, the attitudes of young consumers are well advanced in their new relationship with the medium.

The truth is, these days in many markets it is extremely difficult to build a brand solely on television unless there are unlimited financial resources. The commercial implications of this development create significant challenges for marketers today.

As Nestlé-Rowntree's UK marketing director Andrew Harrison observed in *Brand Strategy*, April 2002, "The fundamental economics of TV advertising now preclude this being the way to launch or relaunch many brands. We have begun to see major UK retail brands across the last decade establish themselves with very little or no TV support."

Advertisers are increasingly contrasting rising television media prices with a reduction in the cost of the raw materials in their products and increased efficiencies in other areas of the supply chain. For example, Harrison contrasted the costs of launching a chocolate brand today compared with 24 years ago. **Each TV rating is today about 13% as impactful, and six times more expensive, than 24 years ago.** In contrast, the average price of Nestlé-Rowntree's chocolate brands today is only three times more expensive than 24 years ago. The economics are clear.

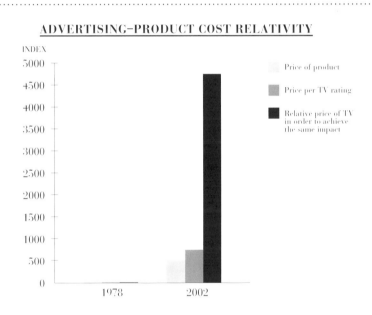

ADVERTISING–PRODUCT COST RELATIVITY

Television is not the same medium it used to be. If conventional communications strategies are employed, the amount of money and effort needed is far greater than ever before, due to fragmentation of audiences, smaller sets of audiences, less frequent viewership, more distractions to commercial audience delivery, changes in consumer behaviour and attitudes, and increased clutter. Consumers have far more choices for entertainment than ever before and these will continue to grow.

Implications for TV media owners are severe. As audiences reduce and fragment, so too will advertising revenues generated from the brands that have traditionally built their franchises through mass television advertising. Both Procter & Gamble and Unilever have reduced the proportion of their investment in traditional mass media communications, primarily television, and increased their spend in other areas such as digital media and experiential marketing.

They are not alone.

In the US, the share of brand owners' overall marketing budgets accounted for by traditional below-the-line disciplines — such as CRM, sales promotions, public relations and sponsorships — increased from 30% in 1990 to 70% in 2000. Given the spiralling costs of advertising media, this trend is likely to continue.

The UK demonstrates how the exponential growth in media channels causes fragmentation. This picture is replicated throughout the majority of the world's reasonably sophisticated markets.

The challenge for TV media owners is to find new revenue streams: new advertisers from new sectors, increased revenues from product placement and sponsorship, and — with the advent of digitalisation — new uses for the medium such as off-the-screen inquiries and purchasing.

....

GROWTH OF MEDIA CHANNELS OVER RECENT YEARS IN UK

MEDIA CHANNEL	1975	1985	1995	2000
Commercial TV Stations	1	2	59	283
Commercial Radio Stations	16	49	160	292
Print titles	NA	6868	8532	8863

SOURCE: Industry estimates

Television is a prime case of a mass medium no longer being "mass". Historically, there were only ever a handful of stations in a typical market. Competition was fierce and stations always tried to offer "something for everyone". The media owner had one screen, one platform, and he had to attract as many people to it as he could. Now in American cities, and increasingly in Asian markets, there is a channel for everyone; channels that broadcast nothing but sport, nothing but news, nothing but cartoons, nothing but history, nothing but shopping. The same is happening across the world — different stations are pegging out different segments, and each segment is specific but inevitably smaller.

Television's greatest strength is at once its greatest weakness. The very nature of the medium makes it the primary focus of the audience's attention. But when TV advertising intrudes into the main content every 15 or 20 minutes, it interrupts that focus and can become an irritant. (In the US, TV commercial breaks now occupy 16 minutes of every prime time hour, and 20 minutes of every hour in daytime programming. And compared to the 1960s, commercial breaks are now three to four times longer.) Occasionally commercials will go to air that interest and stimulate an audience, but by and large most ads do not. The end result is that viewers increasingly try to avoid them.

In some markets, ad avoidance on TV is running at historically record levels. 45% of respondents in the *SENSOR* survey said they try to avoid watching TV commercials.

TV – ADVERTISING AVOIDANCE

Which of the following types of advertising do you personally try to avoid most?

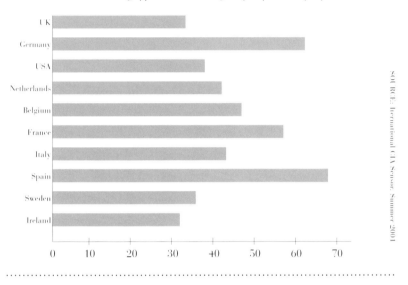

SOURCE: International CIA Sensor, Summer 2001

Even if a brand owner runs a highly creative "break-through" commercial, there is still no guarantee it will be seen — and certainly not in the numbers indicated by industry research.

More opportunities to avoid commercials are now available to consumers. In some European markets and the US, a recently developed device called TiVo records television in real time. Viewers can actually watch a programme ten minutes after it has started, and use the fast-forward facility to skip the commercials. (Interestingly, research among TiVo owners showed that around 80% use the skip function. The ads they skip vary by sector — with the definite exception of beer commercials!)

Paradoxically, while TV is the medium where people most want to avoid advertising, it is also the medium which 53% of respondents cited as their

TV – ADVERTISING INSPIRATION

Which of the following types of advertising do you find most useful
for giving you ideas for things to buy?

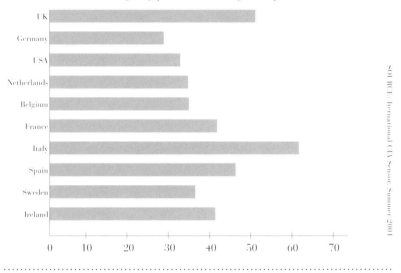

SOURCE: International CIA Sensor Summer 2001

primary source of inspiration about things to buy.

Clearly, a contradictory relationship exists between consumers and television. They know that some of the stuff is interesting, but there is an awful lot of it that is not. And because TV is delivered in real time, and time is the one commodity that consumers have identified as their most precious, audiences have demonstrated that in many cases they are not prepared to sift through all the dross to find the gems. In a world where consumers are financially rich but time poor, why should they?

Which brings us back to the old method of FMCG advertising — creating one execution that is then blitzed to consumers with hundreds of TV ratings. It no longer works, at least not nearly as effectively as it used to. Marketers are far better off with a fewer number of ratings and a much more specific message going into programming that is

CURRENT ADVERTISING RESEARCH SAYS THESE PEOPLE ARE WATCHING YOUR AD.

WHO'S REALLY GETTING SCREWED?

Current advertising research is breathtakingly inaccurate, because its methods are outdated.

For instance, it says that people in the same room as a switched-on TV are always watching the TV. Whereas even common sense will tell you that they sometimes have other things on their mind.

This is just one way current media research misleads clients when it comes to judging the reach – and hence the effectiveness – of their advertising.

We can tell you of others. Because we've put together a report which documents the failings of existing media research – and which suggests a radical, but practical, alternative.

Please find enclosed a summary of our revolutionary report. But we'll happily send you a copy of the full document if you ring George Michaelides, our Head of Media Strategy, on 01-436 3333.

Alternatively, take another look at the picture above. Is that what is happening to your advertising budget?

HOWELL HENRY CHALDECOTT LURY, 16/17 MARKET PLACE, GREAT TITCHFIELD STREET, LONDON W1N 7AJ absolutely right for the target audience, rather than trying to be all things to all people all the time. **In much the same way that there are no longer any mass brands, so too has the "mass" nature of television diminished.**

Marketers need to thoroughly understand their consumers' relationship with the medium generally, and with programmes specifically, and how open they are to conventional advertising approaches. It is fair to say that those products and brands that are aimed at "mass" audiences have a better chance of being seen by their target audience. Lower, older demographic groups are inclined to be heavier TV viewers and so absorb messages. However, the more upstream or youth-oriented a brand is heading — and the reality is that more brands and advertising are moving upstream or aiming at youth — the harder it is to actually connect with those audiences.

Is it smarter for marketers to use a greater variety of executions to overcome the irritation factor? In other words, keep the viewer rewards coming to keep viewers entertained and interested. Certainly that makes sense in terms of keeping the interest levels up, but the other problem that marketers face is not just the quality of their own work but the quality of everyone else's. If everyone else's ads are boring, and theirs run later in the break, then the audience may have already been lost. Creative techniques to keep audiences interested have to be married with innovative media buying tactics. One view propagated is that being first in a commercial break, or first and last in the break so the message spans the break, can grab the audience's attention before it dissipates. But once the audience has "gone", it does not matter how good the creative was. If the audience is not there, it is academic.

Is money the answer? Should marketers treble their budgets to offset lost exposures, assuming of course they could afford to do so? While it is more profitable for media owners, media specialists and advertising agencies if clients spend more money, the answer is no. In fact, it is not so much a question of spending more money, but rather one of employing the medium in ways that reflect their consumers' relationship with it. A marketer can take a very small proportion of his TV budget and invest it to gain insights into his audience, their perceptions of brands, and how these both inter-relate with media channels. He should first establish the benchmarks, especially the current level of brand awareness and saliency, and his audience's intention to purchase. By measuring the result after the communications programme has been completed, he can determine what his investment achieved. Were objectives achieved? Was intention to purchase positively affected? And what happened with that fundamental determinant of all success — sales? Because each brand's DNA is different, each market sector is different, and consumer interactions with each brand are different, these insights and measurements build up a bank of learning for the future. Over time, a picture of what is required to achieve the desired brand objectives will emerge, and a virtuous circle will have been created.

Changing the television dynamic is one solution available to every marketer. After 50 years, the industry still sells — and marketers and agencies still generally think in terms of — 60 seconds, 45 seconds, 30 seconds and 15 seconds and then buy 800 rating points delivering 80% 1+ coverage at an average OTS (Opportunity To See) of 10. Why? An average OTS of 10 means that some people will see the advertising once while others will see it over 30 times. Even the norm these days — an effective coverage of between 3 to 5 OTS — means that many people will still see the advertising far too often. Fear of change, and the lack of willingness to embrace change, contribute to this current inertia.

Occasionally, the dynamic has been challenged. The advertising industry has upheld the Apple *1984* commercial as a creative icon. It is generally ranked the best TV commercial ever made in America. It launched the Apple Mac and only ran once — in the 1984 Super Bowl telecast, a programme that historically attracts over half of all American homes. It was a huge idea, inspired by George Orwell's novel and directed by Ridley Scott: a lone girl destroys the image of Big Brother much to the horror of his assembled clones. Ever since, the commercial has stood as a beacon of bravery, creativity and innovation both in terms of the creative execution and the bold, unprecedented media strategy.

A decade on, another shrewd marketer re-engineered the *status quo* of television. First Direct in Britain was launching a bank without branches, a radical marketing concept that was given an equally radical media and creative execution by UK-based agency Howell Henry Chaldecott Lury and their media specialist partners. Anticipating consumer apprehension about an "invisible" bank, two different commercials were aired at the same time on two different channels. Viewers were told they could watch the "Optimistic" view of the new bank on one channel, and the "Pessimistic" view on the other. First Direct refused to accept the television advertising environment of the day and set about creating its own.

With all the technological advances since then, it is surprising that more creative and media breakthroughs of this magnitude have not been achieved.

Embedding advertising messages into the content is another means of communicating with self-editing viewers. When we know that viewers turn their attention away from commercial breaks, surely it makes sense to find ways to embed the brand message into the content that the viewer has specifically chosen to watch. The embedded message has to be relevant to the content and must be executed in a way that is sympathetic to the programme environment.

It might be as straightforward as product placement in TV shows and movies — BMW and Perrier in the James Bond movies, FedEx in Tom Hanks' *Castaway*, or GAP in *The Minority Report*. Product placement is set to become one of the fastest growing areas in marketing. Already, major content producers have grasped its massive potential, tapping directly into brand marketing budgets worth hundreds of billions of dollars each year. Twenty companies such as Ford, Sony Ericsson, Omega, Revlon and British Airways supported the marketing of MGM's James Bond movie *Die Another Day* to the tune of US$120 million in exchange for having their products seen in the film — a staggering sum considering that the movie cost MGM only US$100 million to produce! (And certainly, a situation that invites some interesting conclusions about "James Bond" as a brand.)

TV stations covering sports events now have the technology to superimpose paid-for brand messages over the signs and hoardings around the arena. They can even locate them centre field. Virtual advertising means marketers can digitally insert on demand whatever they want — signs, products, packs, shopping bags — into dramas and sitcoms. Advertising and programme content integrate seamlessly. It may well be tampering with reality, but as long as it does not distort what they are watching will people accept it? Consumer advocate Ralph Nader's Commercial Alert organisation in Washington DC says virtual advertising is another good reason why people ought to be giving up their TV sets. So, is message embedment simply more manipulation of consumers by advertisers and the media — or is it a legitimate alternative to commercials? The jury is still out.

Screening commercials without interrupting the programme was a brave experiment conducted in the UK by Sky TV (known as Star TV in Asia). Commercials were screened in a portion of the screen akin to an Internet banner ad while the programme carried on, the idea being that the audience would not have their viewing interrupted. In theory, it allowed the advertiser the benefit of involvement with the programme in such a way that his commercial would be seen.

The tests were controversial. How much attention would viewers give those messages, and would they prove even more irritating than the traditional commercial break? Advertisers were cautious at first, but once data was released showing a 10-15% increase in viewing it became a sought-after route for dealing with ad avoidance.

Screening commercials without interrupting the programme: a brave experiment by Sky TV in the UK.

The point remains that despite these new and ever evolving dynamics, few have ever really challenged the value of television advertising until recently. Certainly no one has been able to measure the real value of audience delivery on a consistent basis. If television is to maintain and grow its revenue streams, this will have to change.

Press

Interestingly, the *SENSOR* survey revealed that readers of newspapers were far less likely to try to avoid advertising in newspapers. In fact, only 6% of the overall sample consciously avoided commercial messages.

The key word here is "consciously". Arguably, readers do not feel the need to consciously avoid press advertising as much as ads on television, largely because the nature

NEWSPAPERS – ADVERTISING AVOIDANCE

Which of the following types of advertising do you personally try to avoid most?

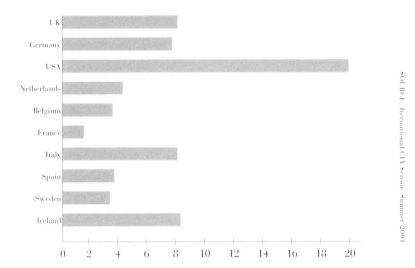

SOURCE: International CIA Sensor Summer 2001

....

NEWSPAPERS – ADVERTISING INSPIRATION

Which of the following types of advertising do you find most useful
for giving you ideas for things to buy?

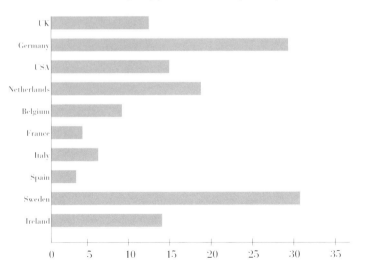

SOURCE: International CIA Sensor Summer 2001

of the medium allows them to edit out what they are not interested in anyhow. They can simply do what newspaper readers have done for centuries — turn the page. Press advertising is not as intrusive as television advertising. Nor does it interrupt the consumption of the news, unless the reader decides to divert his attention.

When the sample was questioned about the value of newspapers as a source of ideas for things to buy, 15% of respondents indicated newspapers were their primary source of inspiration.

Despite the predictions that newspapers are "yesterday's medium", they still have a tremendous role to play. One of their traditional and existing strengths is their convenience and portability.

Magazines

Because cover prices are often expensive, primary readers have relatively intense relationships with magazines. The primary reader will be strongly connected to the content and is likely to savour every aspect of it. If a marketer's message is relevant to that reader, the opportunities are very powerful.

However, magazines sell advertising space based on their total readership. The big monthly glossies can claim up to 10 readers per copy. While primary readers have an intense relationship with the magazine, the same cannot be said for someone who picks up a copy in a dentist's waiting room for a 10-minute flick. But the way magazine advertising rates are often priced, both readers are treated with equal importance.

MAGAZINES – ADVERTISING AVOIDANCE

Which of the following types of advertising do you personally try to avoid most?

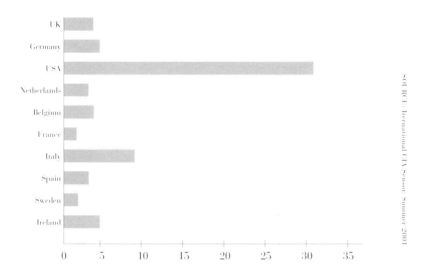

SOURCE: International CIA Sensor, Summer 2001

....

MAGAZINES – ADVERTISING INSPIRATION

Which of the following types of advertising do you find most useful
for giving you ideas for things to buy?

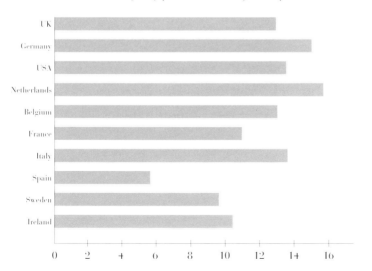

SOURCE: International CIA Sensor, Summer 2001

The *SENSOR* survey scored consumer magazines strongly when it came to advertising avoidance: only 6% of readers actively edited out the ads.

The theory that magazines are bought for product information gained further support: 13% of respondents cited magazines as their primary source of ideas about things to buy. No doubt if this were analysed down into specific groups, notably young females, the percentage would increase significantly.

Magazines enable tighter communications with specific groups when they are in a receptive frame of mind. *Vogue*, a perfect example, has become virtually a catalogue of fashion advertisers and for some women, this is the primary reason they buy it. Women are looking for new trends, new colours, new technology for skin care; they are absorbed in all those developments. In Asia, where particularly young women see cosmetics as more of a necessity than a luxury, the companies that market these products have taken approaches much more akin to FMCG marketers than luxury goods companies. Interestingly, many luxury goods advertisers now complain regularly about "clutter" and how difficult it is to stand out from the competition in women's titles.

Very often advertising executions are created in Paris, New York or Milan and used globally to deliver consistent brand messages wherever the ads are seen. For example, the Louis Vuitton Moët Hennessy Group markets up to 16 main brands across Asia-Pacific with the creative work done in Europe. The creative conventions of fashion and cosmetics advertising are rigidly adhered to; most ads feature a full or double page photograph and the brand name. Headlines and copy are a rarity. As a result, advertisers have to work hard to get their ads to stand out from the rest. One notable exception is the recent launch of YSL's M7 fragrance for men. The use of full frontal male nudity created at least as much attention in the news media as it did in paid-for advertising.

Gatefolds, tip-ins, the use of thicker paper, and book-marking (so the magazine opens to a specific ad) are becoming media conventions in themselves, so much so that some cover gatefolds can be irritating for the reader. Double-spreads can be impactful, but are also very easy to avoid.

The editorial integrity of magazines is a frequently debated issue. When consumers look to magazines for genuinely objective advice on "best-to-buy" items in different categories, how can they trust print titles that sell their souls for the advertising dollar? As many media owners now rely more on advertising revenue for their profit, advertisers can influence the skew of a story. This influence is often exerted indirectly. The size of a contract might be enough to silence any adverse criticism.

Radio

It is tempting to consider radio as more an ambient medium than "mass". By its very nature, radio is highly personal. Like TV, radio advertising is intrusive and an interruption of the content, which means it can easily irritate. While listeners are unlikely to switch stations, they certainly resent hearing the same execution repeated four times an hour. Very often, station promotions are the worst offenders and do a severe disservice to paying advertisers.

The *SENSOR* survey supported this argument with only 9% of respondents stating that they actively try to avoid radio advertising. However, there were indications that listeners have a tendency to subliminally edit out messages if they are not of interest.

Media specialists would generally advocate tailoring creative executions to specific audiences. The execution that runs on morning drivetime will not necessarily suit the ambience of late-night programmes, or the mood of Sunday morning listeners. Creatively, radio offers rare opportunities to develop an outstanding campaign idea with multiple executions. In most markets, an entire radio campaign can be recorded and broadcast for considerably less than the production cost of a typical television commercial.

3% of survey respondents found radio useful for getting ideas for things to buy, confirming that messages on radio tend to be more subliminal.

How effective is radio nowadays? In 1999-2000, a Millward Brown International tracking study in Britain commissioned by the UK Radio Advertising Bureau concluded that adding radio to TV had a 15% multiplier effect. In other words, if 10% of a given TV budget was re-deployed onto radio, the campaign's overall efficiency in building awareness increased on average by 15%. When radio was used in isolation, it was measured to be three-fifths as effective as television at raising awareness levels, but did so at around one-seventh the cost. Interestingly, the study revealed evidence of misattribution: consumers thought they had "seen" a campaign on TV when radio was the only advertising medium used in their market.

RADIO – ADVERTISING AVOIDANCE

Which of the following types of advertising do you personally try to avoid most?

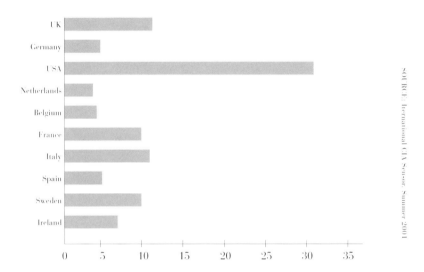

RADIO – ADVERTISING INSPIRATION

Which of the following types of advertising do you find most useful
for giving you ideas for things to buy?

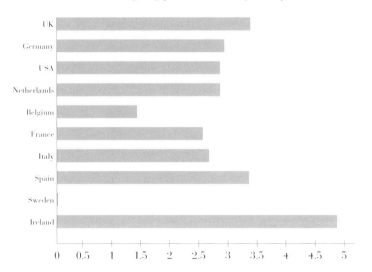

Cinema

Cinema is somewhat of an anomaly. Historically, it has tended to be creatively more interesting in developed markets because of the sheer impact of the big screen combined with state-of-the-art digital sound systems. And because FMCG companies rarely use the medium, there tends not to be the clutter normally associated with television. In rural areas of the less-developed Asian markets it remains a primary source of entertainment and information. The incredible size and continued growth of the Indian film industry bears testimony to this.

The cinema audience is captive and facing the right way. They have chosen and paid to be there. The audio and visual dynamics completely absorb them.

Marketers have the opportunity to be very creative both with the execution — and within the environment itself. Saatchi & Saatchi London once created interactive cinema for British Airways. An actress was planted in the audience. She leapt up and started arguing with the characters in the commercial, which had been carefully timed and shot to allow for two-way dialogue. Shocked at first, audiences were soon enthralled by what was happening. When the "commercial" ended, resounding applause filled the cinema.

SENSOR revealed some significant differences between American and European cinema audiences. US cinemagoers were religious in their avoidance of the ads, mostly cheap slide announcements for local advertisers — some 35% saying they actively avoided these commercial messages. In the markets of Europe, the figures were considerably

CINEMA – ADVERTISING AVOIDANCE

Which of the following types of advertising do you personally try to avoid most?

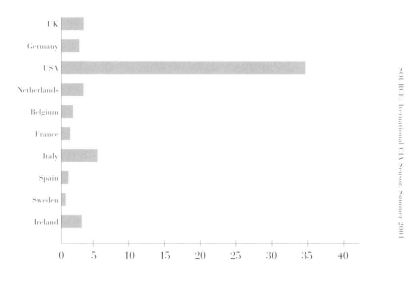

SOURCE: International CIA Sensor, Summer 2001

....

CINEMA – ADVERTISING INSPIRATION

Which of the following types of advertising do you find most useful
for giving you ideas for things to buy?

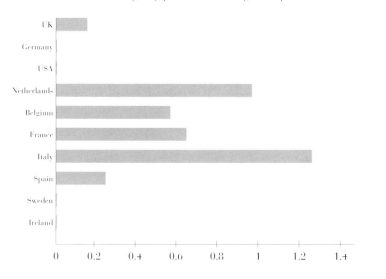

SOURCE: International CIA Sensor, Summer 2001

lower. (In fact, British audiences happily turn up early at the cinema specifically to see the ads, something that Americans think is crazy.)

Cinema scored low on the inspiration for purchase issue, reinforcing the belief that cinema is perceived as an entertainment medium, rather than an informational one.

Outdoor/Out Of Home (OOH)

Arguably, outdoor is the world's oldest advertising medium (having promoted the world's oldest profession on the walls of Pompeii). And today, conceivably it is the last truly "mass" medium. Generally it remains very difficult to accurately measure audiences of outdoor advertising. Nowhere is this more true than Asia. On the surface, the numbers are seductive. But while the number of cars and people passing a poster site is impressive, there are many other things they are paying attention to.

The *SENSOR* report indicated that as with radio, the level of respondents who actively try to avoid OOH advertising is generally low at 7%. Which is to be expected; it is perfectly simple for consumers to edit out OOH messages simply by paying attention to other things going on around them. It is not normally intrusive, nor does it interrupt the consumer's primary activities.

As might be expected, OOH scored very low in terms of providing consumers with ideas for things to buy. Only 3% of respondents cited the medium as informational.

The research backs up one of the major concerns about outdoor's efficacy as an advertising medium: it can literally become part of the scenery, and in so doing become invisible.

OUTDOOR – ADVERTISING AVOIDANCE

Which of the following types of advertising do you personally try to avoid most?

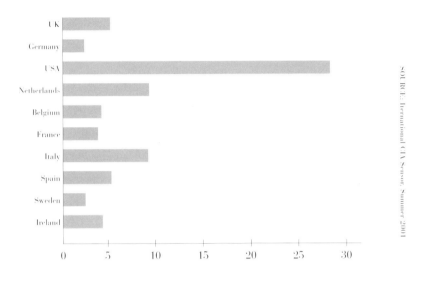

SOURCE: International CIA Senent, Summer 2001

....

OUTDOOR – ADVERTISING INSPIRATION

Which of the following types of advertising do you find most useful
for giving you ideas for things to buy?

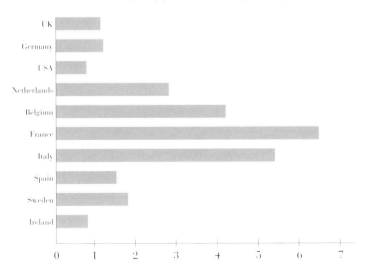

SOURCE: International CIA Senent, Summer 2001

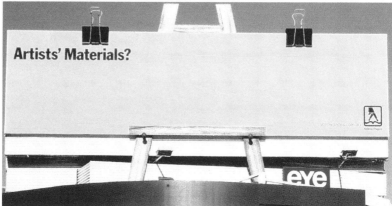

Excellence in outdoor: Clemenger BBDO Melbourne for the Yellow Pages.

It is all too easy to take it for granted. Poster sites, 24-sheeters, transit billboards and neon signs are mostly there for what is optimistically called "reminder value". The trouble is, they are generally so static and passive that we need reminding they are there in the first place.

Where outdoor excels is when a car is "glued" to a poster, or an aircraft's wheels have supposedly clipped the top of a billboard, or some element of the poster moves (such as a massive tea bag being dunked endlessly into a cup, or electronic tickertape news flashes).

NON-TRADITIONAL NEW MEDIA
On-line
After the madness of the dot.com boom, on-line marketing has settled down into a more realistic pattern and offers some powerful opportunities.

The *SENSOR* survey ranked the Internet third after TV and radio in terms of ad avoidance, with an average 8% across all markets. Distinct differences emerged: 16% of American respondents found it more intrusive, with Europeans generally less bothered. This is not surprising as the US is a more mature market for on-line and so ad clutter and consumer "fatigue" were more evident. It is worth noting that reducing click-through rates on banner ads around the world have tended to follow US trends especially as the novelty wears off.

Clear evidence existed that consumers saw the Internet as an immensely valuable source of ideas for things to buy.

One explanation for the apparent disconnect between the two charts is that on-line consumers prefer web sites of their choosing rather than have one thrust upon them by advertising. When people do connect to a marketer's web site, they are much more likely to be highly motivated, highly interested, and of course, unlike most other media channels, the on-line consumer has the opportunity to make an immediate purchase.

Interestingly, despite its specific, tightly measurable audiences, on-line advertising has always lacked the appeal of shotgun mass media. For example, banner ads have come in for a lot of criticism, and some of it fairly so. Yet not only can the number of people who click onto a banner ad be measured, it is also possible to track how much time they spend on the ad, whether it leads them going through to the web site, and whether that eventually leads to a transaction. According to European digital marketing service leader Outrider, a realistic expectation might be that 0.3% of the potential audience will actually click onto one.

But because the measurement of banners offers such a small response, it is generally assumed they are less valuable than conventional advertising. In reality, however, it is rarely possible to say how many people pay attention to conventional media.

Ambient media

While the concept is not necessarily new, the name "ambient" is. The definition of an ambient medium could, in a word, be "Anything", or perhaps "Anything else". Anything appropriate that can deliver an advertising message. Anything you can write on, draw on, paint on, or hang something on. Anything you can borrow or subvert to deliver a brand

ON-LINE – ADVERTISING AVOIDANCE

Which of the following types of advertising do you personally try to avoid most?

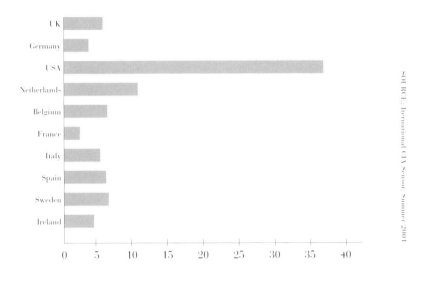

SOURCE: International CIA Sensor, Summer 2001

....

ON-LINE – ADVERTISING INSPIRATION

Which of the following types of advertising do you find most useful
for giving you ideas for things to buy?
(compared with Internet penetration)

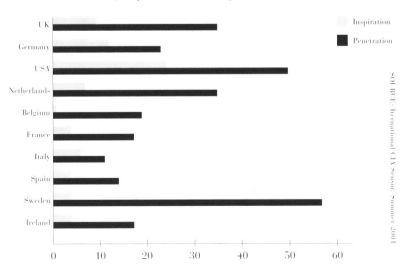

Inspiration

Penetration

SOURCE: International CIA Sensor, Summer 2001

contact. Even a team of men "pushing" a bus once delivered a message for a New Zealand energy drink.

Ambient techniques are surprisingly old. In *Advertising Advertising*, Winston Fletcher reports how in nineteenth century Britain, ingenious advertisers came up with all sorts of new media. *Lloyds Weekly Newspaper* advertised on coins. Pears' Soap advertised on the back of postage stamps. Leaflets promoting tooth powder were distributed over London by exploding artillery shells and some bright spark even invented a shoe that could be used to stamp brand logos on pavements. Concerns about advertising clutter were shared by earlier generations. In 1861, some 1.15 billion handbills were being distributed every year in London alone. William Smith, a market researcher of the time, established that during a walk through London the average pedestrian would have 250 handbills stuffed into his fist. As one media expert in those days commented: "Any man can stick a bill upon a wall, but to insinuate one gracefully and irresistibly into the hands of a lady or gentleman is only for one who, to natural genius, adds long experience."

The sidewalks of New York were arguably the first ambient medium of recent years. Over a decade ago, agency Kirshenbaum Bond & Partners used street stencils for a small client, Bamboo Lingerie. A cheeky message, in politically correct washable paint, appeared overnight on the sidewalks outside department stores: "From here, it looks like you could use some new underwear. Bamboo Lingerie." It literally got under women's feet — and definitely under their radar.

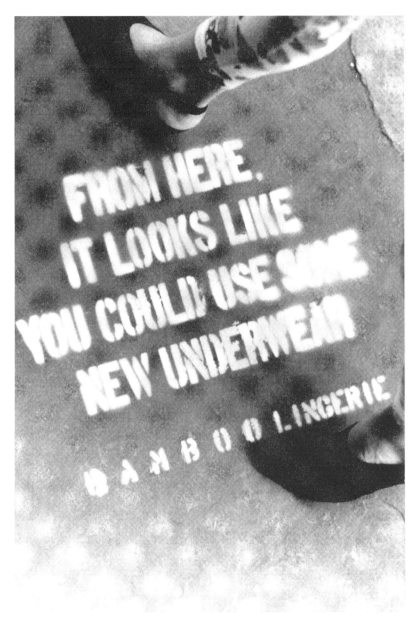

The defining ambient message of recent years: Bamboo Lingerie's street stencils by Kirshenbaum Bond New York.

Two distinct forms of ambient media have evolved. **Structured ambient media** are shopping trolleys, supermarket floors, laser projection onto buildings, balloons, dirigibles, car park boom gates, bike ads, taxi ads, and many, many more.

(Opposite) Washing a pair of "knickers" in a transparent taxi top: Lowe & Partners Singapore for Brandt Group Asia.
(Above) Demonstrating leg room for British Airways, by M&C Saatchi Singapore.

Meanwhile, **unstructured ambient media** is the whole area of creating your own medium; there are no rules to that, beyond local government restrictions. Anything can be ambient — like a fountain gurgling red blood (red dye, actually) to promote a TV horror movie, or the creation of lung-shaped ashtrays by DY&R Wunderman on behalf of the Singapore Cancer Society.

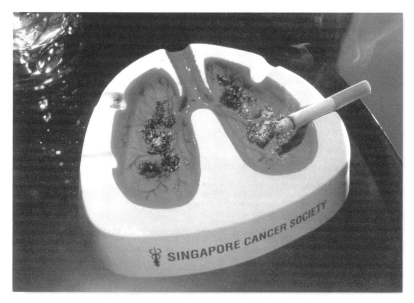

Anything can be ambient: DY&R Wunderman for the Singapore Cancer Society.

Creative brilliance for TV3 movies by Colenso BBDO Auckland.

By definition, ambient media is rarely plagued with direct clutter. Because the marketer has created his own environment, he has excluded anyone else from being in it. His message has exclusivity, and exclusivity is power. The question is, how do we put an empirical value on an uncluttered environment?

Take one of the best examples of unstructured ambient media that recently won the Media Award at the Cannes International Advertising Festival. The organisers of a Brazilian drink driving campaign had persuaded the leading bars in the major cities to have drink-drive messages stuck to the bases of beer glasses. As drinkers finished their beer, they looked down into the glass and saw the message staring them in the face. Whoever would have thought of the bottoms of beer mugs as an advertising medium?

If ambient is so potent, should marketers arbitrarily allocate a percentage of their advertising budget for it — even though the medium might not as yet have been created? There is no fixed formula, and "off the peg" solutions are dangerous. Increasingly though, a media strategy for the more innovative and sophisticated marketers — depending on their product and objectives — could well contain a significant amount of ambient media.

It would be unlikely for any marketer to attempt a national ambient campaign. **As a rule of thumb, the more ground a campaign has to cover, the value delivered by ambient media diminishes.** It is far more likely that a very rich ambient campaign would focus on a few cities where the core consumers reside. Where a marketer has a high concentration of the target audience, and when a very rich interaction with the brand can be created. ambient offers a far more valuable interaction than any "opportunity to see" from conventional media.

Very often ambient will be more than advertising. It will be an opportunity for sampling, for demonstrating — something that goes beyond just delivering a message. In a Singapore ambient media success, Evian mineral water wanted to announce a new bottle that young adults could hook onto their belts when they went clubbing. The conventional solution would have been to launch it with an ad in young adult magazines. But as far as young clubbers were concerned, a conventional ad would have been passive, predictable, and surrounded by clutter. Something outside the normal context of advertising, something "in-your-face", would be more interactive and thus more relevant to them. So dozens of new Evian bottles were suspended from the ceilings of pedestrian underpasses which carried high volumes of young people to the trendy clubs of Singapore. After calculating the cost of labour, permission fees, and a creative fee for doing it, it worked out, roughly speaking, the same as the conventional media route. The new bottle was the ad. It spoke for itself. If it could hang from a ceiling it could hang from your belt. Seeing it literally 360 degrees, 3-dimensionally, achieved a more powerful impact on consumers than a flat image on a magazine page. It was out there where the audience was, creating a buzz, conveying some sort of elitism — whereas an ad in a magazine would have been an ad in a magazine.

A word of caution: ambient rose to prominence by

inspiring clever, amusing, inventive creative opportunities. Now there are 400 specialist ambient media companies in the UK offering a range of unconventional media from bananas to coffee cups, pizza boxes to urinals. As the ambient sector becomes more popular, marketers should be wary of the madness of fighting clutter with uncreative ambient solutions that simply add further clutter.

Point Of Sale and Supermarkets

Many brand owners have redirected advertising investment from television to in-store — but in a much bigger way than conventional banners and shelf-talkers.

Nestlé-Rowntree's UK marketing director Andrew Harrison believes **supermarkets are a new medium in their own right**. In *Brand Strategy*, April 2002, he argued: "If I want to get a message cost-effectively to 70% of British households in a week, do I plan a centre break in a peak-time soap or do I run a display end in Tesco? It's clear that in-store, at point of purchase, will have a greater impact… We're learning that trade marketing activity can build brand equity. Watch out for the retailer — TV's true competitor."

Will supermarkets become the new mass medium? The division between the retail distribution channel and media communication channels is fast disappearing. They are all just channels now, to be judged on their relevance for connecting brands with consumers. Tesco marketing director Tim Mason endorses that view: "We want media buyers to think of us as a media channel." Meanwhile, the US-based retail giant Wal-Mart recently declared that it expects to become the world's largest media owner by 2010, just seven years from now!

Given fragmenting media audiences, the supermarket offers accountable communication with vast numbers of interested shoppers. It answers the problem of tighter budgets, especially when nearly 40% of US grocery brands have close to no funding for traditional media advertising. And it is a marketing environment where it pays to be seen: unplanned purchasing decisions made in the store can amount to 60-70% of an average supermarket visit. Johnson & Johnson called it: "Collaborative customer relationship management, where retailers merge their knowledge of the shopper with manufacturers' knowledge of the consumer."

Today's leading supermarkets are more than sales promotion environments. **They are environments of trust.** The best supermarkets in the UK, the US and Australia are strong brands in their own right, often stronger than the well known manufactured brands on their shelves. They are creating brand experiences out of their stores.

Retailers not only control consumer access to brands, today they increasingly own the consumer relationship. They are total communities in which the relationship between the consumer and the supermarket as a brand is often far stronger than the relationship between the consumer and the manufactured brand. In fact, UK supermarket brands like Tesco and Sainsbury's now sell petrol, issue their own credit cards, and offer a range of financial products. And the list keeps growing. They are creating genuine communities, leveraging the trust that exists between them and the consumer, not dissimilar to the way Virgin has developed a whole raft of different businesses out of the Virgin brand.

The challenge for marketers is compelling. Many retailers' own-label brands are now stronger than well known manufactured brands. Retailers' own-labels now score well on quality and trust, once the sole preserve of the traditional brand. In some markets, own-label brands have penetrated to over 50% share of certain categories. For traditional brands to remain leaders, they must continue to lead through innovation, differentiation and quality. Power brands and niche brands still have the opportunity to thrive, but the threat from retailers' own-labels may prove too great for brands in the middle.

It is still early days, but industry predictions include changes in manufacturer-retailer relationships, changes in manufacturer marketing communications strategies, and retailers treating their supermarket "mass medium" as a profit centre.

Presently only a handful of supermarket brands in Asia have achieved consumer relationships of this strength. But because the UK, the US and Australia generally lead the marketing world, the implications and opportunities for Asian marketers are massive.

Mobile Communications

Arguably no other piece of technology has wrought such change in social behaviour as the mobile phone. In Asia incessant mobile phone calls today have reached epidemic proportions. Outwardly mild-mannered people think nothing of having loud conversations in cinemas, or disrupting meetings, plays and church services to take calls. Pre-concert announcements, inflight messages and signs in hospital wards have failed to stop them. Mobile phone boors have even been gaoled for beating up anyone who protests their insensitivity.

In a short space of time, SMS texting has become the preferred means of communication for many young Europeans and Asians. Older Asians are following suit. It is a cheap, very fashionable way of communicating and exchanging messages on an interpersonal level. **Ironically, SMS as a new form of brand communications has already scored heavily in terms of irritation.** Unwanted, irrelevant messages are sent to subscribers. Ask any mobile phone user who receives a barrage of messages from telecom providers whenever he lands in a new country.

Chapter 7. AN IMPERFECT INDUSTRY

Our ideas will have to be...broader than advertising alone. We will have to expand our skillset and broaden our mindset.
M T RAINEY

Having explored the new relationships between brands, consumers and media channels, one question remains: how is the marketing services industry organised to cope with them?

In September 2002, *Enders Analysis* observed: "The last three years have seen huge concentration in the marketing services industry. One source suggests that 56% of the world's advertising billings now pass through just seven buying groups, up from 32% in 1999... At the same time, media planning and media buying have moved to the centre of these groups after a century of being little more than a clerical activity at the periphery of their business."

What happened?

The media revolution began quietly enough. Within 30 years, the well-established traditional process of the advertising world would be challenged like never before.

Cats Among The Pigeons

It all started in the 1970s in the UK when visionaries like Chris Ingram — and other media entrepreneurs as far afield as Canada, Australia and France — opened their doors as media independents.

They were totally independent of advertising agency ownership and they believed passionately that media as a function was far more important than the subservient role it was being given within agencies. Their initial proposition was simple: they could buy media for less and manage the process at lower cost. But deep down, they shared an almost unspeakable belief that one day the media function would supersede creative as the lead strategic aspect of marketing communications.

At first, the long-established advertising agencies dismissed the media independents. Their business model was all wrong. They could never profit from their meagre margins. Nor could they provide the one thing that mattered and made the difference to a brand's success: creativity. Therefore, the ad agencies were able to convince themselves that they were doomed to fail.

In those days advertising agencies "owned" marketing communications, and had done since the early 1900s. Beginning on Park Row, New York, where all the major newspapers were concentrated, the first ad agencies were sales agents for media owners from whom they received their commissions. Inevitably the likes of James Walter Thompson and George Batten began designing print ads and posters for the clients who had bought spaces from them, and the ad agency business model grew from there. (In fact, as print advertising proliferated, warnings were issued about advertising's harmful effects on taste, morals and mental health.)

Over the years, as the concept of "brands" germinated and grew, the creative expression of brands to consumers through advertising became more and more important. Gradually, the primary function of these sales agents evolved from acting on behalf of newspapers and periodicals to working for a series of "clients" for whom the advertising copy was the all-important factor. Media sales, the original basis upon which these businesses were built, became increasingly secondary. Over time, it was relegated to an internal administration function. It fell into the category of a foregone conclusion; media planning in those days was hardly rocket science — there were so few choices and all the commissions automatically ended up in the agencies' pockets anyhow. Agencies underinvested in it. More and more, it was treated as the poor cousin to creativity and failed to receive the level of attention that it should have done.

The New Importance Of Media

In the 1970s, a new breed of agency media buyer appeared around the world. These shrewd traders began making a real difference to their clients' advertising budgets. They negotiated heavy discounts and higher quality airtime. These highly paid mavericks thrived on their reputations for aggressive business tactics. Media vendors often feared them, and for good reason. Legends abounded. Their tantrums saw equipment hurled from their offices. TV sales reps suspended upside down out of windows, and screaming matches down the phone, much of which was fuelled by long liquid lunches.

By the early 1980s, advertisers themselves were taking a different view of media. It was becoming more of an issue to them. A deciding factor was the development of more and more quantitative research data. At last, the measurability of media delivery provided an opportunity to make some attempt to understand the return on their advertising investment. At the very least, it provided the chance to learn a little about what they were getting in return for their significant television advertising budgets.

The first media independents faced a lot of opposition. They were regarded as the punks of the ad business. In fact, a member of Britain's advertising industry body, the Institute of Practitioners in Advertising, reputedly described them as "the arsehole end of the world". Chris Ingram, whose specialist media agency Chris Ingram and Associates (CIA) had started up in 1976, later recalled that, "When we started, the agencies tried to kill us and deny us commission. We started because agencies were not investing [in the media function]; they did not think media was important enough." (In 2001 when WPP bought Tempus, the holding company of CIA, for £432 million, Ingram benefited to the tune of £64 million.)

At first, progress was slow. By 1985, spending through media independents represented less than 10% of the UK market. Their growth was faster in Europe, especially in France where Carat emerged as the most influential media specialist. Carat was run by the spectacularly successful Gros brothers, one of whom at one point was the world poker champion.

Through to the late 1980s in Europe, more and more clients began moving the media element of their business out of traditional full-service agencies and started working directly with media independents. By and large, advertising agencies remained indifferent to these changes. By the time they sat up and took notice, the die was cast.

Liberating The Client

At first the media independents dealt with clients whose marketing communications activities lent themselves naturally to media-centric services. Typically, music, fashion and perfume companies produced their advertising at head office, often without conventional agency involvement, and used the same executions regionally or worldwide. Any company with a universal creative proposition saw media — not creativity — as the differentiator. Media efficiency and cost savings thus became the new marketing communications imperatives.

The media independents negotiated directly with their clients, sometimes including a performance element related to their buying and negotiating ability. Of the standard 15% media commission, 10-12% was usually rebated to the client. The media independent retained between 3-5%, an impossibly low margin by the standards of the major creative agencies. Additionally, media independents might retain 20-50% of any savings created by their services, the balance of which was also rebated to the client. The savings were determined by simply measuring the price that the client had paid for each medium prior to having the media independent's involvement. If the media independent negotiated 40% cheaper rates than the client had paid previously, it retained 20-50% of that 40% and rebated the balance.

Because the media independents only provided the media function, they lived or died purely on their ability in this arena. Not surprisingly, they had to become very good at marketing the importance of media. And because the facts were compelling, clients responded with interest. Their argument was simple and effective: clients spent 80% of their budgets in media, but it would have been quite extraordinary if they had ever given the subject 10% of their time and attention. Now priorities were changing. As time progressed through the 1980s into the 1990s, the development of new technology, cable TV, satellite TV, the plethora of new communication channels and the growing sophistication of audiences led to a situation where effectively reaching the consumer became increasingly challenging.

Despite the dire predictions of traditional agencies, media independents flourished. Clients were delighted. They were buying media smarter and getting it for less. And beyond that, the media independents were proving to clients that it was workable to have two different companies running two different parts of what was then their primary marketing communications function.

The "Unbundling" Phenomenon

Meanwhile, media executives based in the traditional full-service agencies started to react to the success of the media independents. They put an increasing amount of pressure on their managements to allow them to break away from their parent ad agencies and form their own versions of media independents. It was a gamble. By taking this step and "unbundling" their media departments, the agencies reasoned, their clients would not appoint an outside media company, but keep their business within the agency's two discrete divisions. "If you can't beat 'em, join 'em" became the mantra of the 1990s.

The first media specialist of this genre was Zenith Media. Born in the UK out of the Saatchi & Saatchi and Bates media departments, Zenith was extremely successful. Before long all the other significant agencies followed suit. With some relish, the industry labelled these companies "media dependents", because at their inception they were largely dependent on their mother agencies for their portfolio of clients. Today, every major multinational agency has an operational media company in one guise or another.

Over time, the collective term for media independents and media dependents became "media specialists".

Rejuvenating Creativity

Interestingly, the advent of the media independent was not all bad news for the evolution of advertising agencies. Not only were clients liberated, but so too were a new generation of creatives eager to break away from their large, long-established and somewhat grey employers and set up their own shops.

In the early 1980s, Britain saw waves of new creative agencies establish themselves. For creative hotshops like Gold Greenlees Trott and Bartle Bogle Hegarty, the media independent gave them the springboard they needed to start in business. For a new agency venture, it was becoming increasingly expensive and difficult to have a media department, attract the right talent, fund media research, and invest in computer equipment —let alone stump up the bank guarantees necessary to gain accreditation with media owners. But by partnering with a media independent, agency startup costs were slashed, and immediate credibility in media servicing was provided.

As a result, the media independents were a crucial factor in the advertising industry's ability to rejuvenate itself. More than a quarter of a century later, media specialists are again enabling a new generation of creatively driven agencies to set up shop, this time in Asia-Pacific.

The Asian Experience

In Asia the development of media specialists spawned a precarious dilemma for the big multinational agencies. Their Asian networks had been losing money on and off for years. They had been established to satisfy global clients — a matter of "you plant your flag where we plant ours" — and expanded with the growth in globalisation. They were a costly investment. When head offices in New York and London began demanding that their Asian offices become profitable, many did — until the mid-1990s. When media specialists arrived in Asia, the agencies' hard-won revenue streams diminished. Back to square one.

Nor were smaller, locally-owned agencies spared. Many had routinely provided "free artwork" to their clients, secure in the knowledge they would make up the loss through their media commissions. Overnight, the swings and roundabouts were removed.

The first multinational media independent on the scene was CIA, opening CIA Pacific in Hong Kong in 1993. Chris

Ingram described it as "a listening post for the markets of Asia", recognising that the markets were not quite ready for the concept of media specialists, but soon would be. Few realised how vast the changes would be, and how swiftly they would happen, in the world's most economically and socially dynamic region.

CIA's joint venture with Batey Ads in Singapore followed in 1996. **Significantly, Asian clients did not ask for media independents.** In fact, when CIA and Batey Ads first presented to their shared clients, few could really see many benefits from having a media specialist work on their business rather than the agency's previous media department.

But once the floodgates were opened, there was no turning back. Others soon followed. Zenith was created out of the media departments of Saatchi & Saatchi and Bates, OMD out of DDB, TBWA and BBDO, and Starcom out of Leo Burnett.

When CIA was developing its Asian presence in earnest from 1996 onwards, its biggest fear was *not* that full-service agencies would adopt the 30-year-old European model and hive off their media departments to create media dependents. Rather, the concern was that they would see the future and take the dramatic, innovative step of hiving off their *creative* departments. Needless to say, they did not adopt that model.

By ignoring the radical opportunity to hive off their creative departments and develop agencies that specialised in communications and media planning and implementation, Asian advertising found itself following the rest of the imperfect world. And because the industry had to grapple with a raft of challenging business conditions unique to the region, it became even harder to achieve commercial success.

Meanwhile, CIA moved in the other direction. It believed that the media discipline should be involved far earlier in the communications planning process than ever before, added strategic planning to its repertoire, and worked more closely on the creative aspects of a client's business. As early as 1996, the more visionary clients in Asia had become increasingly open to the argument that the construction of the media plan should be considered *before* any decisions were made on the creative execution. And that once agreed, the media plan should form the basis of the brief to the creative departments of their agencies.

COUNTRY-BY-COUNTRY AD SPENDS IN ASIA & JAPAN 2000

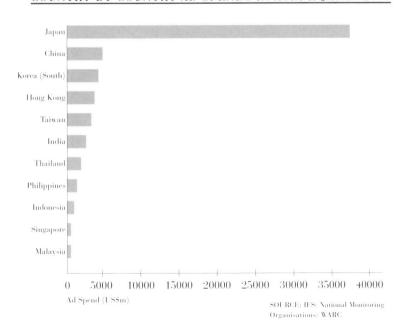

SOURCE: IFS: National Monitoring
Organisations: WARC

When the newly formed media specialists worked with advertising agencies, they would normally agree on a split of the standard 15% media commission. Typically between 10-12% went to the agency, the remaining 3-5% going to the media independent. All of the other revenues — like service fees and production markups — remained the agency's prerogative.

In addition to providing the media planning and buying functions, the media independent would also do the billing, collect the revenue and media commissions, retain its share of the commissions and pass the remainder to the agency. Arguably the media independents worked for far less than they should have done; their share of the work was far greater than the 3, 4, or 5% they were getting. They operated on very tight margins. (In fact, the audited accounts of media specialists suggested they were in the business of money management — through necessity, they made as much money out of managing the money as they did out of being paid for their services.) Indeed, the situation reflected the fact that agencies still "owned" the main elements of the client relationship.

Not surprisingly, clients started asking agencies to be more accountable for the revenues they were earning. Many agencies argued that the "unbundling" being forced upon them in Asia by their global headquarters in New York, London and Paris was tantamount to amputating a limb. The full-service agency model, they said, was a well-balanced machine built around complementary processes of account planning, creative and media (very much in that order) and other necessary support services all driven by the client service teams or as they are known, "the suits". Privately, agencies blamed media specialists for the extreme pressure on their margins and believed it was strategically wrong to separate the creative and media processes. When all the services had been bundled together, their clients had found it difficult to understand the internal cost breakdown. Unbundling media spurred client demands for accountability. Advertisers now expected discounts on everything, from service fees onwards. In fact, one senior regional manager of an agency group operating in Asia-Pacific was quoted as saying that the advent of media specialists was akin to "a scourge of plagued rats infesting our shores".

In all probability, everyone was right. The unbundling of media from ad agencies has without doubt led to all manner of new pressures within the client-agency relationship. At the same time, agencies had failed to read the writing on the wall and recognise the need for prioritisation and investment in the media function. The dynamics of capitalism, economics and the inexhaustible human desire for evolution all coincided to create a new energy that wrought dramatic change and caused the most significant restructuring that the advertising industry had ever witnessed.

The Madness Of Agency Commissions

As time went by, debate shifted to the fundamental of agency remuneration — the agency commission itself.

The original *raison d'être* of advertising agencies — as agents selling space and time for media owners and being paid a "sales commission" — begged many questions. For one thing, advertising agents sold space to their clients —

and if an agent is in business to "sell" not "buy", where do his loyalties lie? Even long after the original dynamic had changed and agencies saw themselves more as creative agencies building brands for their clients, **third-party media owners still provided their basic income**.

Oddly enough, many clients were still quite happy for their partners and advisers — the agencies — to be paid by their media suppliers. With time however, the contradiction became more uncomfortable. The whole commission system was totally in conflict with clients' best interests. The more they spent in commissionable media, the more revenue their agency enjoyed. (Even 20 years ago, at around US$300,000 for a global double-page colour spread in one of the newsweeklies, a 15% commission delivered a US$45,000 income and a good marginal profit.) And the really big budgets, especially those in the huge markets of the US and Japan, produced the really big profits. Fuelled, too, by creative ambitions, big commissions propagated the "big ad" syndrome, just as 60-seconders perpetuated a similar myth on TV. The business issues of an agency and the commission structure became totally counterproductive and counterintuitive to what needed to be going on in the twenty-first century marketing communications environment.

Nowadays, more agencies are persuading their clients to change to fee-based remuneration. More and more clients are embracing the idea. It is a major step towards accountability and understanding what they get in return for what they pay.

The Imperfect Agency

In the Chinese proverb, a frog is put into a pot of cold water and a fire is lit under the pot. As the temperature of the water slowly rises, the frog does not notice any change until it is too late and it is boiled to death. There is a risk that a similar scenario exists for many of the advertising agencies operating in Asia. The changes around them have not happened overnight. They happened over a period of 30 years or so, accelerating especially in the last five years.

Left with just their account service and creative offerings, advertising agencies now have to come to terms with the reality that they are no longer in the business of media.

As such, it has become increasingly inappropriate for the creative advertising agency to pre-empt the entire communications channel planning process when advertising itself might represent only one channel.

Agencies are grappling with two fundamental issues. Firstly, their whole business construct remains driven by the fact that they have massively expensive creative departments. Like any business with a costly machine, that machine has to be kept at full production if the business is to run profitably. Obviously agencies need to sell creative ads, especially television concepts, because that is what these creative machines are geared to produce. And this in turn is a potential source of constant conflict if agencies want to sell something to clients which clients may neither need nor want in today's marketing communications context.

Secondly, the future of the agency account management department — structurally and operationally — remains ill-defined. Certainly it is duplicating a service that media specialists now increasingly provide — that of media account management and planning. If advertising agencies and media specialists are both providing account management services, there is a very clear duplication of costs. This is further exacerbated by the fact that both the creative agencies and their recently formed media dependents are running two distinct (and, in many ways, duplicated) distribution systems across the globe.

The reality is that advertising (like many other branches of marketing communications) is not a profession, it is an industry. Despite the fact that clients around the world entrust over US$300 billion every year to advertising agencies, media specialists and the like, there are no professional barriers to entry. It is not like law, medicine or architecture where five or six years of intensive education are required before an individual is qualified to practise. Arguably, advertising is more akin to real estate in the sense that anyone can do it.

Where Does Creativity Fit?

Once it was always simple, always TV or print. Crafting beautiful imagery was the game. Today, a different reality prevails.

The nub of the problem is the very definition of the word "creativity". In most mainstream ad agencies, creativity means the work produced by the creative department. And in agency creative departments, the focus on creativity by definition is narrow — a craft focus. Occasionally planners, but more often account service deal with the "bigger picture", the strategy, while the creatives roll up their sleeves to do the concepts and execution. The creative process still comes first, as though it were still the single point of difference for a brand. Conventional thinking still dictates that the execution of an advertising message should be the same everywhere, and should be forced into the mind of the consumers regardless of the media environment. The assumption is that single messages are still appropriate to large numbers of consumers. In today's context however, that assumption is false. Laswell's communication paradigm is outmoded.

Because of all the changes brought about by the convergence of technology, consumers' attitudes, the time they have to spend with media, and the fragmentation of audiences, the whole dynamic has completely flipped.

The media environment is absolutely relevant to the consumer's mindset and their willingness to absorb messages, and therefore that must be fundamental to what is being conveyed through advertising or any other form of communication.

As Sergio Zyman reminds us, "Every single thing that happens with your brand, and around your brand, says something."

Many industry leaders argue that creativity requires a broader definition and application. Creativity, they point out, should refer to an agency's intellectual capital across the board.

In Sir Martin Sorrell's view, "Increasingly clients will be looking for creative strategies…creative ways of leveraging their corporate brand strengths; and **creative ways,** not just of generating ideas but...making creativity actionable."

Kevin Roberts, chief executive officer of Saatchi & Saatchi London, put it quite bluntly: **"Advertising must lose its obsession with ads."**

Clients want humility, innovation and wisdom from agencies, argued Melanie McMillan of The Brand Business, in *Admap* July/August 2001. "They require energetic, responsive agencies that use diverse communications channels, comprehensive research, less formulaic solutions..." However, McMillan's survey of Australian clients and agencies revealed a crisis of legitimacy for the creative agencies exacerbated by an "agency obsession with glorifying creativity regardless of results... Clients were vocal in their criticism of agencies, maintaining that they are overpaid and populated by grand-standing personalities who won't listen, and creatives who lack business acumen." As McMillan summed it up, "Agencies have lost sight of what they uniquely offer and have yielded to the dominance of management and brand consultancies."

What do agencies uniquely offer? Donald Gunn, formerly Leo Burnett's worldwide director, creative resources, proved that 346 (or 86.5%) of the 400 most awarded commercials in the world, 1992-1995, had worked in the marketplace. His survey covered Cannes, D&AD and such respected local award shows as the British Television Advertising Awards. Clients and agencies submitted the business results of their commercials. Included in the case histories were Howell Henry Chaldecott Lury's first Orange Tango commercial; the big orange man had pushed up sales by 26%, while brand awareness rose from 42% to 72%.

Bartle Bogle Hegarty's work for Levi's notched up a 27% sales increase in Europe. In Australia, The Campaign Palace's work for the Australian Meat & Livestock Corporation had increased beef consumption by US$196 million from a media investment of US$4 million. At the time, Gunn's study provided the global advertising industry with a formidable weapon to promote the value of its creative product. Unfortunately, that opportunity was largely overlooked. A decade on, it is a different world.

Agencies will have to shift their focus, argued McMillan, "from time-and-place bound communication systems and scheduled media events, to time-shifting, instantaneous communications capabilities that can address consumers relevantly and with their consent. They must build strategies around combinations of channels, using media vehicles for their on-target capabilities."

At the moment the whole construct of unbundling is counterproductive to that and the cause of considerable frustration. As a result of agencies becoming disconnected from media and the process of how people interact with media, creatives too have become disconnected from the vehicles that carry their ideas.

The point is that ad agencies can have a "unique offer", and their creativity can make a difference, but not in the conventional sense and not when it remains hobbled by conventional practices. New methodologies, new collaborative partnerships, will have to be introduced. As British agency head MT Rainey sees it, "Our ideas will have to be...broader than advertising alone. We will have to expand our skillset and broaden our mindset."

Sorting Priorities

Unfortunately, media specialists these days too rarely see the creative before they do the planning. Usually they are faced with a *fait accompli* — "Here is the creative, now connect that to the audience" — and are expected to build from the creative out. If the cart goes before the horse, don't expect it to travel very far.

How should we really engage the brand with the consumer?

The planning has to come first. In his excellent book, *Truth, Lies & Advertising*, Jon Steel describes a geographical method of understanding where you are if you are lost, called *triangulation*. The theory goes that if you are lost it is possible to find where you are with the help of a compass, a pencil, and three landmarks that are visible to you and that are also marked on your map. The compass is used to orient the map so that the landmarks on the map line up with the real landmarks that you can see. Pencil lines are drawn on the map as if to join the real landmarks and their representations on the map. The three lines should ideally intersect at a single point, or at least form a small triangle. If your lines do intersect at a single point, that is exactly where you are on the map. If you get a triangle, you're somewhere inside it. Triangulation doesn't work if you can only see one landmark. Two landmarks are better than one, but there is still a huge margin for error. Three are needed to work properly. The whole point of the exercise is that your chances of finding a solution or uncovering the truth are increased as more perspectives are taken into account.

Similarly, unlocking the potential of brands today requires three points. The first is the real nature or DNA of **the consumer**. The second is **the brand**, its relevance and attraction to the consumer. The third: **the communications channels** and their effects on consumer behaviour and brand perceptions. The intra-relationships between these three points of the triangle hold the key to building successful communications programmes for brands.

It is a generally accepted truth that consumers define brands. Never has this been more true than in today's world of educated, cynical, dynamic and self-editing consumers. It is equally true to say that media channels in their broadest sense — the Web, SMS, cult magazines, pop concerts, MTV, Bluetooth technology as well as the conventional media — have a massive impact in determining consumer behaviour. In order to connect a brand with consumers in a way they will find relevant and interesting, the natural conclusion is

THE CONNECTION BETWEEN CONSUMERS, MEDIA CHANNELS AND BRANDS

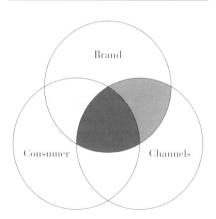

that we have to understand the complex, multi-dimensional intra-relationships that exist between consumers and media channels, and then work out how to fit the brand into the triangle.

So, long before any creative is initiated, we have to analyse the consumer, their psychographics, their attitudes, their habits and their interests, and then decide how best the brand can connect with them – the three Cs: connection, context and content. Media specialists can demonstrate how and when the audience is engaged with different media, and what their mindset is during that period of time. Some obvious examples: Do your target consumers read the newspaper in the morning, and do they read it again during the day, and more importantly what frame of mind are they in at these times? Do they get into the car and automatically turn on the radio? Do they look at billboards when they drive in to work? Do they surf the Net in the office? Do they SMS their friends while they are out? Do they go on-line for gaming or chat? Perhaps they go to the gym and watch MTV and go clubbing to experience the imported deejay? Do they watch TV when they get home? What programmes do they make sure they are home to watch and what do they do during the commercial breaks? By mapping out "A day in the life", we can see when they watch a movie, when they surf the Net, when they play computer games. This form of research or insight is increasingly referred to as ethnography — effectively "watching people" — and is one of the fastest growing areas of qualitative research today.

Out of this will come a communications channel

plan that is solutions-neutral and built around the most potent connection points between the consumer, the brand and the media channels.

Very precise creative briefs can then be fed into the most appropriate communications disciplines to address a range of executional opportunities. Each executional brief will come complete with the consumer mindset. Channel by channel, and medium by medium, creative concepts can address a raft of audience dynamics. **The value of the creative output will be far greater and more relevant, and crucially built around truly valuable connection points between the consumer, the brand, and the salient channels.**

Who Should Run The Show?

The sheer authority of conventional advertising as the key definer of brands is in decline. And ever since that decline commenced, there has been a gap left at the top of the table of influence.

Today, everyone claims that the brand communications process should start with them. Brand design and packaging companies claim that the Nike "Swoosh" is a clear example of why brand design should lead the whole process. From their former territory of supply chain management, management consultants are moving ever closer into the demand chain side of the equation. Advertising agencies maintain their claim to what was their once unchallenged role. Now, media specialists have thrown their hats into the ring as leader of the communication process, along with customer relationship management, sales promotions and public relations companies. All of which can be very confusing for marketers who have to navigate their way around some very effective sales people!

If one accepts that consumer relationships with the media, and the media's influence over consumer behaviour, are the new keys to unlocking a brand's success, then the media specialist has a fair claim to lead the whole brand communications process. In this scenario, communications channel planning would become the media specialist's core competency. However, whether you agree or disagree with that conclusion will most likely depend on your view of what an advertising agency is, and what its future construct will be.

More importantly, what is the client's perspective? The views of clients who have experienced unbundling varies. Some insist that agencies cannot work in isolation and are demanding the reintegration of services — not just advertising and media, but the whole gamut of marketing services disciplines. While as clients they appreciate the new checks and balances they have on media and creative strategies, some are concerned about the negative aspects of the disintegration sometimes created by unbundling.

In fact, Wendy's moved its US$200 million advertising account out of Bates USA not because of unhappiness with the ads, but with the agency's decision to unbundle its media-buying operations to media specialist Zenith Optimedia. Wendy's executive vice president for marketing, Don Calhoon, was reported in *The New York Times*, 16 August 2002, as saying that unbundling was not something that was going to work: "When we're not all at the same table and worried about the same strategies and the execution of ideas, something can go awry. I have to protect the Wendy's brand."

Increasingly, the media specialists are physically moving away from their ad agency parents to strike out for their own independence, developing their own offices staffed with finance and administration people. Without doubt, further additional costs are being added to the overall service. And as we have seen in the Asian context, because clients did not ask for unbundling, many question why they should pay for the extra costs incurred.

What would best serve a client's needs now? The new marketing communications model that is now evolving takes into account the reality that the production of an ad is no longer the brand strategy, but rather the execution of *one component* of the total communications plan. This is a dramatic change that both advertising agencies and clients have to come to terms with. And it begs the question, where should clients go to get their communications channel planning done?

The task will be to retain the consistency of the brand, to protect the franchise that has been built up in terms of the brand's relationship with consumers, and to make sure that the marketing activity takes the new dynamics of consumer attitudes, behaviour and media habits into account. The relationship between the evasive and self-editing consumer and the media will take priority over the relationship between the brand and the consumer. And with good reason. Producing a wonderfully creative piece of advertising is a completely fruitless exercise if it cannot be connected with the consumer in a way that will be trusted, liked, believed and, most importantly, experienced in the most appropriate environment.

Evidence indicates that in some markets the new model is already in place and working now. In one recent example, a major Asian-based global airline very consciously decided that it wanted to have an independent media specialist to help implement its integrated approach to communications and extend its communications effectiveness beyond traditional advertising approaches. As the appointed media specialist explains: "They appointed us as media communications integrators to develop the best communications plan for each desired audience so that the ad agency can focus on brand communications. The agency is the brand guardian, we are the consumer guardian. They encourage us to work together, but in another sense they encourage us to be different, so we can give them our media channel point of view without being subservient to the advertising process. They now want the media function to be partnering the advertising process and disagreeing with it when we feel it's wrong."

THE 21st CENTURY MARKETING COMMUNICATIONS PLAN

Chapter **8. THE NEW DYNAMIC**

Everything you do communicates something about your brand to your customers and potential customers.
SERGIO ZYMAN

The whole dynamic has changed beyond recognition. And it changed more in the past five years than it did in the previous fifty.

Families no longer sit together in front of a television. Kids happily multi-task between different media platforms — both fixed and mobile. "They are not viewers, listeners or readers," said *Advertising Age* in September 2001, "they are users."

Six million bona fide English-language commercial web sites compete for attention. If you asked someone to spend just 10 minutes on only one million of those web sites, it would require 19 years of effort — seven days a week, 24 hours a day.

What Is The New Relationship Between Consumers, Brands And Media Channels?

Technology continues to drive media change. And media change is driving differences in consumer behaviour. The digitalisation of every broadcast media channel will accelerate those changes, as well as accelerate the end of mass media and the rise of greater and greater audience fragmentation.

Even now it has become enormously challenging to reach large audience groups of significant size. As the attitudes, desires and cultures of different demographic groups grow more and more disparate, it is becoming increasingly likely that by effectively reaching one group through conventional media that another group will feel, at best, marginalised and at worse, insulted or patronised. **Whom you *don't* reach becomes as important as whom you do.** This dynamic also manifests itself in the usage of brands themselves. It is not difficult to imagine the damage done to cult youth brands such as Stussy, Vans or Quiksilver if a youth sees a 70-year-old grandmother walking through the streets of Bali wearing a Stussy T-shirt, or an overweight 60-year-old strutting along Singapore's Orchard Road in a pair of Vans, the shoe of choice for skate boarders. (If brands are indeed communities of users, here we have some very extreme gatecrashers!)

The new dynamic challenges marketers to reach out and talk to audiences as individuals. And brands have to react to that. Big brand owners of soap powders and shampoos have already experimented with the Net. Results were mixed, but the point is they explored the connectivity between their brands, their consumers, and this crucial communication platform. The Net is becoming a legitimate way of interacting and building value with your consumer that actually makes sense, provided that the consumer cares enough about your brand to spend valuable time waiting for web sites to download. The fact is that consumers are smarter, more aware, more dismissive and more cynical than ever before, and marketers ignore that reality at their own peril.

If we agree that advertising's primary function is to start, maintain or enhance brand relationships, we can begin to appreciate the full implications of the new dynamic.

Stop Shouting And Start Listening

Consumers define brands, and increasingly media — in its broadest definition — is defining consumer behaviour.

The final conclusion has to be that the relationship between media, consumers and brands is therefore the new dynamic, the new issue. It is no longer about brands deciding what they are and shouting that at consumers. Rather, it is consumers defining brands, media affecting consumer behaviour, and therefore brand owners fully understanding and then achieving a true and constructive relationship between the three.

But have marketers been as smart as they could have been? If they have not been in constant qualitative contact with their consumers, the answer is No. Do they really understand what their brand means to their consumers? Do they know what their consumers like about it and don't like about it? Do they have a planned response that will fine tune the brand relationship and move it on?

Technology And Consumer Power

Today it has never been easier for consumers to choose whether or not they want to interact with a brand. Consumers are very aware of brands. The younger consumers have been surrounded by brands all their lives and they are old enough, savvy enough, to understand what is going on.

They are also better informed. Because of the speed of information exchange, the media can have a very negative effect if a company is discovered doing something morally reprehensible or dubious in manufacturing. More and more famous brands are being scrutinised. Anti-brand anger is on the increase. Nike allegedly using underage labour in Asia made headlines around the world. Consumers voted with their feet. Books like Naomi Klein's *No Logo* challenged the realities of how McDonald's produce their products. Shampoo manufacturers have had to face consumer outrage as a result of testing their products on animals.

There is already some evidence that this new consumer knowledge and power is in part pressurising brand owners to carefully review their manufacturing policies. Reebok is a case in point. Much of its production is outsourced to massive factories in China and, like many other manufacturers, it has been difficult to directly and consistently influence the labour policies of local factory owners. A recent report in the *Financial Times* explained how Reebok put considerable effort into persuading its suppliers to undertake democratic elections of trade union representatives in several of its China-based factories. Thought to be unprecedented in China, these elections were a direct result of pressure on the factory owner by the brand owner. As Doug Cahn, Reebok's director of human rights programmes, explained: "This is not about gaining a competitive edge in the market. I don't know that anybody has bought a pair of Reebok shoes because of its human rights programme. But we're a global corporation and we have an obligation to give back to the communities in which we live and work." While Cahn could well be correct in his assumption that consumers do not find reason just yet to buy products as a direct result of constructive and positive human rights programmes, there is evidence that when human rights and labour abuses are revealed to them, consumers will find good reason not to buy the brands in question and will then use modern communication technology to share the news with growing numbers of other networked consumers.

Increasingly, consumers want to know the social, political and commercial ethics of the companies from whom they buy their brands. In *Fast Food Nation*, Eric Schlosser reveals that "96% of American school children can identify Ronald McDonald, more than can recognise the crucifix." According to Schlosser, fast food companies preach the values of consumer choice and democracy — specifically the right to choose between a burger, a pizza or a microwaved apple pie. Schlosser's point is that the profits of the fast food chains have been made possible by the losses imposed on the rest of society — obesity, food poisoning, rural poverty and environmental degradation. In *Captive State*, George Monbiot argues: "We're faced with a profusion of minor choices and a dearth of major choices. We can enter a superstore and choose between 20 different brands of margarine, but many of us have no choice but to enter the superstore." Meanwhile, anti-advertising groups such as Adbusters creatively defile billboards: Absolut Vodka is changed to read "Absolut Hangover", Ultra Kool cigarettes become "Ultra Fool".

All these developments have a profound impact on the way consumers view brands and their intentions of interacting and purchasing. And they represent the start of a long-term trend towards consumer activism that The Future Laboratory calls "consumanism — shopping with a political and strategic edge."

Because information is now everywhere, consumers quickly reject any brand profiting from what they perceive as practices that contravene their personal values. Brand bullies are even being questioned by "ordinary" people, reports Sean Pillot de Chenecey (alias Captain Crikey) in *AdMap*, May 2001. He observes that over the last couple of years, young children and teenagers have started to show real understanding of the admen's methods and know precisely what they are up to.

Times have indeed changed: now target audiences target the brand. Not only that, they are keen to spread the word within their community. And the new media channels of email and SMS texting, for example, enable this to happen at a speed and with such breadth as never before possible.

The speed with which consumers reacted to the sharksfin issue was extraordinary. Media coverage revealed how sharks were caught, their fins lopped off to provide the delicacy for sharksfin soup, after which the sharks were thrown back into the water to die. Even arthritis sufferers who regularly took sharksfin cartilage tablets to relieve their ailment said enough was enough and binned their tablets.

Consumer Power and the Pressure on Advertising

Consumers have more power than ever before. They are demanding more and more value for money.

It is not just an issue of price, but what else comes with that price. What are the add-ons, the security, the benefits and the after-sales service?

As a result, manufacturers and service businesses are under ever increasing pressure to constantly improve all aspects of the value of their brands while at the same time reduce prices by reducing their cost of doing business. In order to reduce prices, manufacturers and brand owners are putting increasing amounts of pressure on the companies that service them — of which ad agencies are one small factor.

The ongoing battles between advertising agencies and marketers over terms of business, fees and production costs, are partly a reflection of the consumer's demand for better and better value, and cheaper and cheaper prices.

Every percentage point that a client saves on an ad agency's costs can go to his margin, or be passed on as a saving to consumers. It is yet another reason why the dynamics of the client-agency relationship continue to be challenged so dramatically.

What Is Advertising's Place In The New Dynamic?

Jeff Goodby of premier American creative agency Goodby, Silverstein & Partners once compared advertising with architecture. Advertising, he said, is an unavoidable part of the environment. It should be intelligent, humorous, beautiful and moving, "a welcome and respected part of what we all have to walk through every day". Advertising should seek **"the highest common denominators, not the lowest".**

Preceding Goodby, legendary San Francisco copywriter Howard Gossage had argued against the mind-numbing repetition of commercials and the resultant irritation factor. "How many times do we have to read a book or see a movie? Once, maybe twice, even in the best cases. **Why do we suppose that advertising must be seen over and over again to have an effect?"**

When there was little information about new brands and products, advertising was prominent. But today there is information everywhere, more information than consumers could possibly hope to deal with. In an age of information overload, advertising's impact has diminished. And while consumers can still get a buzz from a new commercial, much advertising is greeted simply with cynicism. Increasingly, advertising's role in the new dynamic is governed by a context far bigger than advertising itself.

More than ever before, consumers experience brands in a 360-degree way. And when the brand underperforms, people speak their minds. Sergio Zyman rightly points out that: **"Every single interaction between a brand and a consumer plays a part in defining the brand in the consumer's mind."**

For example, the following joke was e-mailed recently to countless people, many of whom were in all probability frequent flyers:

A guy sitting at an airport bar in Atlanta noticed a beautiful woman sitting next to him. He thought to himself, "Wow, she's gorgeous. She must be a flight attendant. But which airline does she work for?"

Hoping to pick her up, he leaned towards her and uttered the Delta slogan: "Love to fly and it shows…?" She gave him a blank, confused stare and he immediately thought to himself, "She doesn't work for Delta!"

A moment later, another slogan popped into his head.

He leaned towards her again and said, "Something special in the air?" She gave him the same confused look. He mentally kicked himself and scratched American Airlines off the list.

Next he tried the United slogan. He said, "I would really love to fly your friendly skies…" This time the woman turned on him. "What the f--- do you want?" The man smiled, slumped back in his chair and said, "Ahhh, Qantas…"

Of course it is only a joke, but think about the damage this viral message does when it is e-mailed to potentially millions of travellers. It conveys a very negative message about the service aspect of Qantas' brand. It also damages employee morale when they are constantly reminded that their inflight service and attitude is reflective of the joke.

The consumer's relatively newfound sense of self-value and confidence results in more consumers speaking up to complain, to question every aspect of a brand, the manufacturer's ethics, and to share their experiences with their fellow consumers. In *Beyond Disruption*, Robert Birge and Damian O'Malley addressed this changing context: **"The idea that branding is a kind of spin control is dead. Everything a company does is branding… Who cares about a brilliant 30-second commercial if you have to wait 30 minutes in the customer service line?"**

The best brands understand this and consistently perform across every aspect of their delivery to consumers. Consumers may well pay attention to a beautiful airline commercial, for example, and even react to it, but what is of greater interest to them is what happens when they experience the brand themselves. What happens when they check in: how are they treated, what is the lounge like, what is the airport like? What happens on board the aircraft: are the staff gracious, what is the food like, what are the seats like? All these brand interactions can be negated by one bad experience. Using the airline analogy, the first question anyone is asked when they get off a plane is, "How was your flight?" Doubtless it is a rhetorical question, but it is a great opportunity for someone to vent his or her feelings. "Terrible." Damage done. The ripple effect is enormous and way beyond the scope of advertising to correct.

Given the new dynamic — the relationship between media, consumers and brands — what is the way forward?

9. THE WAY FORWARD

Shrewd marketers create change. They do not let change create them.

What If There Were No Marketing Services Companies?
Marketing organisations have to challenge themselves about all their marketing processes, especially marketing communications.

One of the companies that has led the way in this, perhaps not perfectly but certainly with great courage and conviction, is Unilever. They have redefined the role of their media specialists as communications channel planning agencies, and redefined their creative agencies as brand agencies. But does this go far enough?

Brands cannot physically be disconnected from media channels, because the channels so acutely affect the behaviour of the consumers who in turn define the brand.

The real question is:

In this day and age, and with all the changes described earlier in this book, what is the most effective and efficient method for a brand owner to build a marketing communications plan — a plan that will have the best possible chance to deliver the brand's objectives for growth?

The Solutions-Neutral Environment

Ask any client — be it the CEO, the marketing director, the sales director — what their objective is, and they will always say growth.

According to UK-based brand growth specialists Added Value, there are only three ways to grow profits:

1. By acquisition
2. By cutting costs
3. Through organic growth.

Acquisition has its limits; companies can only acquire so much before their hunger runs them afoul of government authorities and anti-trust legislation, or they run out of attractive targets.

Cutting costs is also a limited option; if costs are too savagely cut to the bone quality will suffer, brands will lose market share, and their future will be severely compromised.

The way of achieving unlimited growth is organically. And the only way to grow organically is to operate with open thinking — to take risks and to constantly innovate.

Communications channel planning is all about growing brands and growing the business, and it demands an open-minded, solutions-neutral environment.

First, a word or two about the phrase "solutions-neutral" — or, as it is sometimes termed, "media-neutral".

Taken at face value, the word "neutral" can be read negatively. Addressing this, David Fletcher, deputy chairman of Mediaedge:cia UK, eloquently observed in *Campaign*, 8 November 2002: "Neutral is a dirty word. Neutral is diplomatic, detached. Neutral requires the discipline of consideration. Neutral is the language of containment, compromise, summits and accords which bring agreements which allow us all to carry on doing what we did before. Neutral has all the verve and passion of Switzerland."

Fletcher went on to explain the true nature of solutions-neutral planning: "If this strategy is to provide the intellectual platform for all activities, then by definition it needs to be portable across channels — to be as incisive and effective in each relevant discipline as any single-channel strategy — produced in gloriously focused isolation."

A completely solutions-neutral brand growth approach does not confine the brand to advertising, or customer relationship management, or point of sale. It is purely about what is the best solution, or series of solutions, **built on real insights about the brand, the consumer and their interaction with the media channels**, that are most likely to achieve the fundamental objective of brand growth. And that process, in its purest sense, is the future of how companies should approach the way they look at marketing.

Media commissions are one of the enemies of neutrality. A number of blue-chip clients still demand channel-neutral planning on the one hand, while insisting that their agencies are remunerated by commissions paid by media owners on the other. While brand owners allow their agencies and media specialists to be remunerated by commissionable media, they should not be surprised when they receive recommendations that contain little else but commissionable media solutions. If they want completely solutions-neutral 360-degree brand growth advice, then they will have to remunerate their agencies and media specialists in a way that encourages them to provide it.

Insights: Where Do They Come From?

Insight is an overused and misused word. In the context of communications channel planning, insights can only come from a real in-depth understanding of the consumer, the communications channels that affect consumer behaviour, and how those in combination can affect the definition of the brand and aid its growth. It boils down to obtaining the answers to four simple questions:

1. Who is it that we need to talk to?
2. How do we talk to them?
3. What should we say to them?
4. When and where can we most effectively communicate with them?

Consumer insights are not about the consultant's experience or projecting his particular, subjective points of view. They have to come from what consumers really think and feel about the brand, the brand proposition, and how that relates to them as individuals. Consumer insights have to enable the brand owner and his communications partner to find the most valuable connection or contact points, those that his consumers are passionate about and that will encourage them to interpret his brand in a way that will deliver sustainable growth. **And that can only come through research** — not research in the conventional sense, not focus groups and the like, not something artificial, fabricated by people sitting around a table saying what they think they ought to say, or seeing if they can impress the other people around the table, or who are there simply because they enjoy playing the discussion group game (like the young man we met in *Secret Lives*™) — but research that delivers genuine insights into what is actually going through the minds of consumers.

A few years ago, Levi Strauss needed a fundamental shift in their brand and product profile. Levi's Engineered Jeans delivered that paradigm shift. They were inspired by the result of research conducted not in the conventional, structured way, but in clubs and bars at night when the kids had been partying. Young people were interviewed by other young people who wore the same clothes and shared the same "look". And the truth came out. Armed with that truth, Levi's were able to initiate a series of actions that led to a complete, much needed shift in their business and product focus.

As Jon Steel informs us, **people on the inside of any company assume that all those on the outside share their own level of knowledge of, and enthusiasm for, the company's products**. As Steel says, "it often falls to the planner to break that illusion." Steel is opposed to the "unnatural habitat" in which far too much research is conducted. He advocates **creating a research environment that replicates as closely as possible the place and mood that consumers will be in when they have contact with the brand or its advertising**. For Goodby, Silverstein & Partners, Steel conducted the exploratory and strategic research for Sega's video games in kids' bedrooms. Isuzu respondents were ferried by bus to nearby dealerships. He took families out for the evening to Pizza Hut, researched gin at a hip martini bar, and held focus groups on board a Norwegian Cruise Line ship. For the California Fluid Milk Processors Advisory Board, respondents went without milk for a week to see what effect it would have on their lives. This use of ethnography, in these "real life" interactions with the brand, provides far more value in terms of really understanding the consumer's motivations.

Similarly, BMP DDB London very often gets its insights in people's living rooms. Over the past 30 years, the agency has recruited more focus groups than any other organisation in London, including the major market research companies. It operates its own network of recruiters, and conducts around two-thirds of its qualitative research in homes rather than rooms with one-way mirrors.

Crucial insights may also come from observations about the brand, its competitors, and the marketplace in general. David Fletcher recalls a key insight for the development of the Stella Artois strategy. "Every lager company chases football" was a simple but very important observation. In the UK, lager drinkers were becoming more discerning. It was likely that they would respond positively to an upscale, premium communication rather than the usual stereotype beer icons of football and attractive young women. This immensely valuable insight was born out of a well-structured analysis of competitive strategies and tactics. The end result differentiated the brand simply by not following the pack.

Once I Have The Insight, What Should I Do?

Armed with genuine insights, **brand owners can look at their brands, markets, consumers and communications channels in a more 360-degree way.** Then they will take action on several fronts — especially with the brand experiences they offer.

With communications channel planning, brand owners do not just look at how they connect with the consumer to get the sale. They look at the consumer's full life of interaction with the brand. As Tim Delaney of London agency Leagas Delaney puts it, "What people want from brands these days is different. I don't think that people necessarily want just a selling relationship... It isn't a straightforward transaction. It's much more about an experience, it's much more about the brand being something they can feel the sides of."

Many automotive brands now offer consumers **holistic brand** experiences. It is not just about connecting with consumers in the market for a new car. The brand has to answer consumer questions beyond the sale itself: "What happens when I take it in for its first service? How will I be treated? Will I get a loan car? Will they come and collect my car from home and bring it back? Will I get some sort of preferential treatment? Or will I feel like I'm being overcharged?" The brand experience must begin before they even go to the showroom for a test drive. And it should continue. It should make the car owner feel good about having bought the car *after* they've bought it, so when they come into the market again they will not only buy the same brand, they are likely to upgrade to a different model.

Once I Look At My Brand Holistically, How Might I React As A Marketer?

When brand owners buy into the concept of communications channel planning, by definition they are open-minded. They would have recognised that — for whatever reason — their current activities are not working the way they want them to, that there are gaps and problems with them.

Invariably they would have decided that they needed a sea change in their marketing communications. They would already be planning to stop, or have already stopped, what they were doing. Their intention would be to wipe the slate totally clean and start again. As part of that process, they might have already acknowledged and dealt with some fundamental brand and commercial issues — perhaps flaws related to distribution or point of sale display — that had been long ignored.

Addressing this issue in *Fast Company*, April 2002, Dawn Hudson, senior vice-president strategy and marketing at Pepsi-Cola, was reported as saying: "I want an agency that is creative enough to help me reinvent my whole business. Lots of agencies understand brands and how to reinvent them, but I'm not seeing the kind of big-picture thinking that will help clients take advantage of the multiple ways in which people experience brands."

When they do adopt this approach, and are supported by the right approach to channel planning, marketers will have a new, very clear definition of where their brand really is in the minds of consumers, and what returns can be realistically expected from it. Their new expectations will have been thoroughly quantified. They will have accepted that they need to engage with consumers through a broad range of channels planned to interact holistically, rather than simply deluge them with mass communications. They will understand clearly that inappropriate, glossy, one-way messages to wise, communicative, cynical consumers are not the way to start the brand experience.

Innovation: A Fundamental Component For Success

For many years, the reality has been that few marketing campaigns were truly integrated across all the disciplines and communications channels. This is an increasing frustration for marketers who understand the value of properly integrated brand communications.

In reality, time is rarely taken to infuse the marketing strategy and channel communications plan with true innovation. There might be an element of innovation conferred on the message. By investing time and multi-disciplined resources, genuine breakthroughs in channel thinking can be achieved. (Already we can witness the growth of UK media owners' ideas and cross platform departments.)

In an ideal world, the "creative" — in the conventional sense of it being the product of the creative department of an ad agency — would become creativity, or in a broader sense, innovation. And the responsibility for innovation would be shared by *all* parties involved in the communications planning process, from the brand owner through to the individuals involved in the detail of managing specific executions.

Investment Return On The Communications Budget

Communications channel planning has to be holistic. It is far more involving in the business success of the client. Marketers have to get everything right for it to work — especially positioning, pricing and distribution, but then what's new?

Identifying and setting an appropriate investment return is crucial. Remaining solutions-neutral is key. If, for example, distribution is wrong or incomplete, then the advice of the communications channel planner would be **not** to embark on any consumer promotion until the product is readily available. Today, consumers give brands one chance.

Achieving the desired levels of investment return will be explored in the next chapter. At the heart of it though, the marketer has to understand the relationships that his consumers have with the channels of communication. He will need to take the time and make the investment so he really understands their behaviour patterns, not least because they change so rapidly. The only way he can find out how his consumers are likely to interact at different connection points with the brand is by understanding their attitudes to the brand and their media channel consumption habits and interactions. Once the dynamic of each connection point in his consumer's day is understood, the creative messages that will make those connections interesting and valuable to the consumer can be made and managed.

And again this comes back to the fact that **marketers cannot any longer expect to connect their brand with their audience using one generic creative execution**. The relationship between consumers and media now is so specific, and so changeable, that if a marketer tries to force through the same execution he will at the very least lose value, and at worst cause consumer alienation among certain groups.

Chapter **10.**

NAVIGATING THE MAZE

Planning communications channels will no longer be secondary to creative ideas and development under a new mandatory system called Communications Channel Management... elevating the planning of communications channels to an earlier, more strategic role than decisions on creative work.
UNILEVER SPOKESPERSON,
ADVERTISING AGE, JUNE 2000

It used to be that the formula was simple: build the brand with a strategic advertising campaign, excite the trade with a trade campaign, and devise some tactical activity and point-of-sale to push consumer demand through the trade. And few would have been able to quantify the return on investment. Today a new approach is needed.

As Jack Klues, CEO of the Starcom MediaVest Group, put it in a recent *New Yorker* article: "Once upon a time there were four television networks (in the USA) and a few dozen print publications. That was the palette we had to paint with. Fast-forward to today when there are hundreds of cable networks, thousands of newspapers and magazines, the massive infrastructure that we call the Internet, plus technologies like TiVo that greatly impact our ability to deliver messages." Klues went on to describe how these, along with other changes, have shifted the balance of power. "At the same time, the consumer population has fragmented dramatically, and each group demands programming, messages and entertainment tailored to them. It's clear the balance of power has shifted unequivocally to consumers... they are not tolerant of irrelevant messages."

mediaedge:cia

TRADITIONAL MEDIA ADVERTISING MODEL

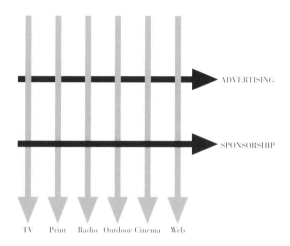

ADVERTISING

SPONSORSHIP

TV   Print   Radio   Outdoor   Cinema   Web

navigator

The traditional media and advertising model was built upon a simple matrix of opportunities based around advertising, and advertising-related sponsorship, cutting horizontally through the six mainstream media. Choices depended upon the specific opportunity and media mix. It involved media planning and media buying.

So far, in today's context, we have talked about channel planning. This raises the next question: once the planning is done, how is it implemented?

Communications Planning and Implementation (CP&I)
The development of the communications planning and implementation (CP&I) process has a short but dynamic history. Perhaps in the same way that the media entrepreneurs of the 1970s believed that the conventional advertising business model was ripe for a new challenge, so too again did a small number of individuals from a wide array of marketing, advertising and media backgrounds three decades later. As discussed earlier, the folk at Unilever played a key role in legitimising its development, not least because they have put a form of it into practice and when Unilever acts, everyone sits up and listens.

Globally there has been a movement by media specialists towards developing a CP&I service. This chapter will focus on one such process branded Navigator™.

Navigator™ is not the only process that has been developed to meet the needs of today's new dynamic. Starcom MediaVest Group has developed a respected channel planning model described as "Impact through Insight". It is linked to a new way of doing business called "Fuelling Brand Power", based on the pivots of unique consumer insights, contact innovation and value creation. Other media specialists also have their own versions of the process at various stages of development.

At the end of 2001, WPP acquired the UK-based global media and branding company Tempus Group plc. When WPP decided to merge the media arm of the group, CIA, with their existing media company The Media Edge to form Mediaedge:cia, they were putting together two companies that individually believed in the principles of communications planning and implementation. More importantly, the new company was determined to take it to the marketplace in a practical form.

Prior to the merger, both companies had independently made considerable progress developing formalised processes that would deliver a CP&I offering to their clients. So it was not surprising that by May 2002, the two companies had merged, analysed each other's CP&I process, and combined the best elements of both to create a proprietary process called Navigator™.

Navigator™ is designed to provide marketers with genuinely objective or solutions-neutral planning and executions driven entirely by the fundamental need of every brand — growth. It eliminates situations where discipline or channel selection is a reaction to an existing creative execution. Everything is born out of the consumer. In this respect, it is ruthless. It requires standing back objectively and asking what is right for the brand, what is right for the consumer, and building a plan from the top down, rather than the bottom up. It enjoys absolute freedom from subjectivity and self-interest, which may seem obvious but is rarely ever the case.

Navigator™ is a journey of discovery that invites the creative collaboration of every discipline. And it is especially intended to work in full collaboration with the brand owner's marketing department and its marketing services partners.

Navigator™, as a CP&I process, reconnects media channels with strategic communications on a much wider scale. It calls for a thorough and open-minded understanding of the three points of the triangle — the brand, the consumer, and all the available channels through all the available disciplines, and their inter- and intra-reaction — in order to relay brand messages and build a dialogue with the consumer. It identifies the best occasions of when and where to connect with consumers, and the most appropriate channels — the how and what.

In this sense, similarities exist with the Starcom MediaVest Group model. As Klues explains, it "seeks to unlock those pivotal consumer encounters, enhance the consumer's brand experience, and strengthen the bond between that consumer and the brand."

Navigator™* acknowledges the fact that every creative message should be a conversation with the consumer, not a one-way shouting match.

By taking a major step upstream from the conventional media planning routes — TV, radio, newspapers and magazines, cinema, outdoor, and trade publications — it thoroughly explores the intra-relationship between brand, consumer and all communications opportunities: CRM, PR, content development, promotions, in fact every possible channel of connection with the consumer.

---

* The models for communications planning and implementation in this book, and the proprietary Navigator™ tools, were developed by Mediaedge:cia, and are currently available to its clients.

mediaedge:cia

THE NEW COMMUNICATIONS CHANNEL MODEL

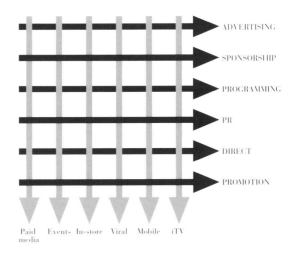

navigator

The Navigator™ CP&I process takes into account how disciplines and channels have evolved, how consumers interact with them, and how they now work together.

At the core of the process is the principle that all communications development starts with the consumer, and that all discipline and channel solutions precede and influence the development of creative messages.

Creativity should not be at the beginning or the end of the process, but should osmose through every strand of the process through to the final detail of implementation across all platforms.

While on one hand Navigator™ challenges all prejudices and assumptions, on the other it reintegrates all the disciplines and influencers in the process — including the client — with the consumer at the epicentre of all thought development.

mediaedge:cia

NAVIGATOR 4 I's SUMMARY CHART

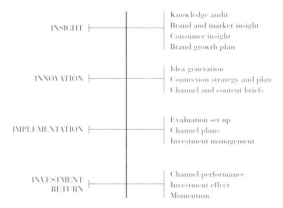

navigator

··

The Navigator™ process is built around four phases known as the four I's:

- **Insight**
- **Innovation**
- **Implementation**
- **Investment return**

By enabling the communications planner to get far closer to every element of a client's business, the process delivers a virtuous circle of objective, solutions-neutral, consumer-centric brand growth. It measures investment returns and learnings, and this in turn allows the process to restart from a heightened level of awareness and knowledge.

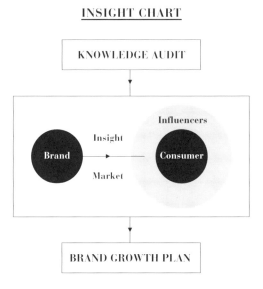

mediaedge:cia

INSIGHT CHART

KNOWLEDGE AUDIT

Insight
Brand → Consumer
Market

Influencers

BRAND GROWTH PLAN

navigator

The First I: Insight

The process begins by unlocking the consumer opportunity for brand growth.

Step 1 is the knowledge audit and briefing process. All available data and information that already exists within the universe of the parties involved will be gathered and sifted — market brand sales volume and value, regionality and seasonality issues, promotion and distribution issues. How much share of mind does the brand have against the market? What were the tracking results of previous activity? In broad terms, what is the overall picture? And further to that, where are the important gaps in knowledge and how best can they be filled? Often, this will result in the commissioning of bespoke research programmes designed to unlock further insights and to fill gaps in the existing knowledge base.

Steps 2 and 3 develop a full, mutual understanding of the brand, market and consumer dynamics.

Working from the brand perspective, the channel planners will probe the client's existing perception of the brand essence, brand vision, and positioning. What rational and emotional benefits does the brand deliver to the consumer? Connected to this will be a full understanding of the market dynamics: in what direction is the client's market heading? How is it segmented? What is the competition doing? And how does competitive activity manifest itself within the channel dynamics?

Next on the agenda is the penetration of the brand and the profiles of its consumers. Consumer analysis will investigate their lives, needs, motivations, attitudes, habits, behaviour, media and brand usage, barriers to brand adoption, brand relationships and consumer passion points. This deep understanding of the client's target consumers will be the springboard for the brand platform and planning brand connections. The channel planners will have gained greater levels of insight into both the client's category of business and his target consumers. Category insights will allow them to sort out the deliverables by probing key decision drivers, segmentation typologies, new sources of business, and marketing communications opportunities. All knowledge will be tabulated.

This process enables channel planners to look for and find opportunities for the brand to break the category rules.

This complete understanding of the connectivity between the brand, the market and the consumer enables planners to identify the first set of key performance indicators (KPIs). They will be fine-tuned later in the process.

Step 4 is the final stage of Insight and develops the brand growth plan. This stage becomes highly collaborative with the client and discipline specialists in terms of scoping, agreeing and validating the specific objectives, and reaching accord on the feasibility of the budget in broad terms. This is an important point as it is often the case that the budget provided by the client to achieve the brand's growth objectives needs to be challenged and reviewed against the agreed scope of work.

medaedge:cia

SUMMARY OF DELIVERABLES FROM INSIGHT

| Validation of objectives |
| Role of communication |

| Current and future source of business | Consumer segmentation, attitudes and motivation |

| Brand positioning and usage | Behaviour triggers and passion points |

navigator

....

From here it becomes possible to collectively validate the marketing communications objectives and agree the overall role of communication. Once done, this again leads to the identification of further concrete and measurable KPIs and strengthens the accountability of the whole process.

mediaedge:cia

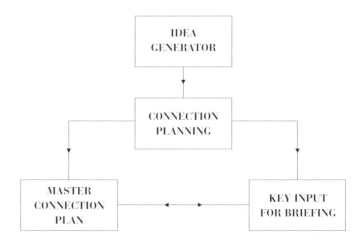

INNOVATION

navigator

The Second I: Innovation

This stage of the process is tasked to deliver **breakthrough connectivity**.

A highly sophisticated and structured brainstorming session, using proprietary methodology called Generator™ developed by UK-based brand consultants Added Value, creates the initial energy.

It is highly collaborative. Typically the brand owner's marketing team, ad agency creatives, and channel and discipline specialists will attend. It is a managed process of creativity born out of a collective understanding from the Insight stage. The facilitator keeps everyone on strategy and more often than not, the session generates a raft of ideas and concepts.

mediaedge:cia

OUTPUTS FROM IDEA GENERATION

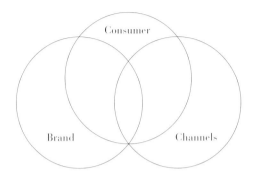

1. Connection
Theme/s and Points

2. Connection
Ideas and Opportunities

3. Channel and
Discipline Objectives

navigator

What breakthrough ideas have emerged?

What opportunities for genuine strategic and channel planning innovation do we have?

Typically, connection opportunities could lead to three broad areas of potential innovation:

1. The creation of a new channel
2. The use of an existing channel or discipline in an unexpected manner
3. The use of existing channels in a different way.

mediaedge:cia

CONNECTION STRATEGY

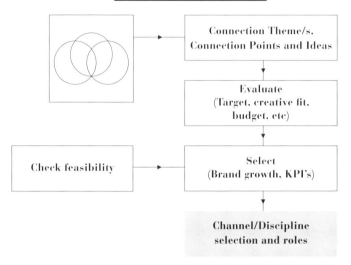

navigator

At this stage, the results of the Generator™ process are evaluated against the brand's positioning through a series of challenges:

- **Is the idea unique and ownable?**
- **Is the environment appropriate?**
- **Will it involve the consumer?**
- **Does it differentiate the brand from its market competitors?**

Finally, the cost/value equation is addressed against the brand growth plan and KPIs.

Channels and disciplines are selected. Their individual and collective roles are defined.

mediaedge:cia

MASTER CONNECTION PLAN

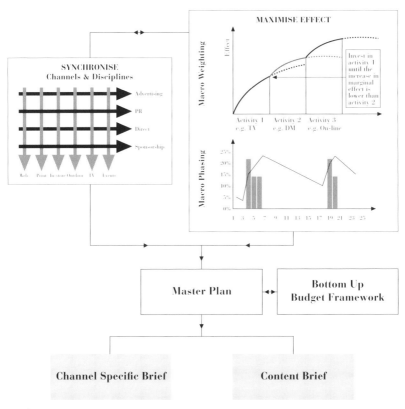

navigator

Channel-specific communication briefs are next developed to synchronise all marketing communications activity — advertising, sponsorships, promotions, PR, internal activities, customer relationship management, digital and more.

Cross-channel impact and efficiency will be calculated through macro weighting by channel and by target audience, and macro phasing to determine whether activities should be continuous or in specially timed bursts.

A bottom-up budget framework emerges.

mediaedge:cia

DELIVERABLES FROM INNOVATION

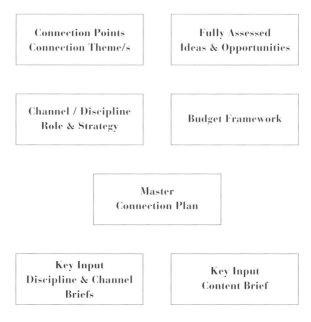

Connection Points
Connection Theme/s

Fully Assessed
Ideas & Opportunities

Channel / Discipline
Role & Strategy

Budget Framework

Master
Connection Plan

Key Input
Discipline & Channel
Briefs

Key Input
Content Brief

navigator

Specific channel briefs are then presented and discussed at interactive sessions with the relevant specialists: the brand owner's advertising agency, PR company, promotions company, customer relationship management company, and the client's internal communications executives.

The critical marketing communications path and customer acquisition models are determined. Will the creative be pre-tested and post-tested? The research architecture, methodology and a schematic for activity are agreed in accordance with the KPI objectives. Research suppliers are sourced, briefed, evaluated and commissioned.

Significantly, the creatively strong service companies from all marketing disciplines are far more excited by working to a brief that has come through this process, rather than one where they have to basically create the whole process themselves. All too frequently, the pressure on creatives to literally "brief themselves" is huge, whereas channel planning liberates them to focus on the actual creative work with a clear and commonly agreed understanding of what has to be achieved — and why.

When clients do not have the appropriate marketing services companies already in place, the right partners are sought from each discipline to manage and implement the work that fits the plan.

mediaedge:cia

IMPLEMENTATION

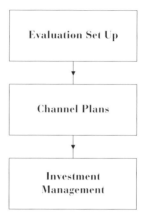

navigator
....

The Third I: Implementation

Now the brand's most potent connections with the consumer can be fully exploited through the negotiation, placement and management of every channel plan.

mediaedge:cia

CHANNEL AND DISCIPLINE PLANS

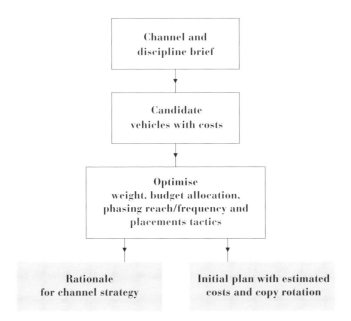

navigator

The connections are mapped. Various discipline approaches will be fully detailed (for example, PR in print two weeks before Internet pop-ups), charting the weight and phasing within each channel, the candidate vehicles and the vehicle mix, and the most appropriate tactical creative and marketplace opportunities.

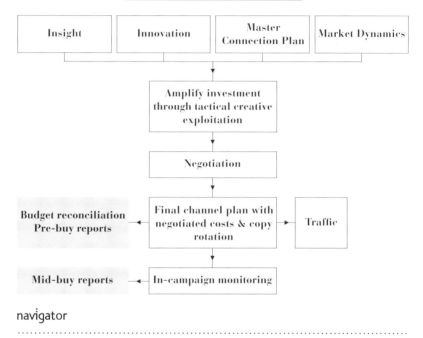

All activity is managed in line with the agreed KPIs.

Negotiations begin. The final channel plan including negotiated costs and copy rotation is tendered for approval.

Day-to-day campaign adjustments will continue against target consumers and in the context of day-to-day trading conditions.

Channel content production goes ahead. (In this context, production has to be part of return on investment. Channel planning would not try to be too specific about individual production budgets, but it would look at the scope of the communications required and seek expert advice on the sorts of budgets that would be likely. Creative recommendations would be factored into the return on investment forecast.)

mediaedge:cia

INVESTMENT RETURN

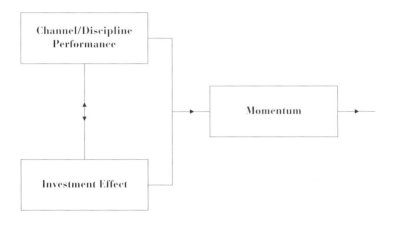

navigator

The Fourth I: Investment Return

This stage addresses **accountable and measurable results**, something clients around the world have been demanding for decades.

mediaedge:cia

CHANNEL/DISCIPLINE PERFORMANCE

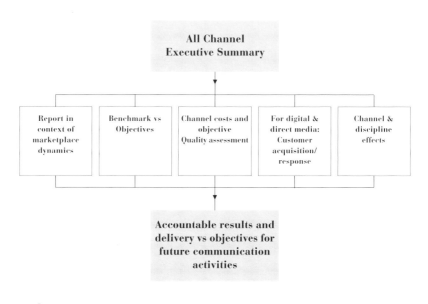

navigator

Each channel and discipline is subjected to a performance review at least annually, depending upon the nature of the activity. The findings become a knowledge bank for future activity. In this way, channel planning can arm brand owners with a powerful weapon in helping to **forecast returns on investment** for future activity, based on clear, measurable results.

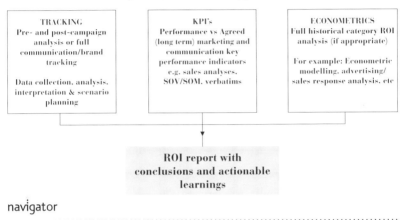

Three general, non-exclusive routes can measure the brand owner's return on investment:

1. Pre- and post-campaign analysis using brand tracking studies, sales analyses, customer acquisition data and verbatims
2. Performance rated against agreed marcom KPIs, using data collection and interpretation
3. A full historical category return on investment analysis using econometric modelling, awareness modelling, and response analysis.

These KPIs are, effectively, a quantitative expression of the objectives. All learnings from each discipline and channel, and their implications, become actionable for the next marketing communications planning cycle. What worked, what did not? Where do we need to think again? What did the competition do this time? How will they react next time?

How can we outflank them next time around? Return on investment is an ongoing process. The more continuity there is, the better everyone becomes at it.

The Navigator™ process is particularly important and valuable for clients who face internal pressure to justify marketing communications budgets. Forecasting is tough at the best of times, but if the channel planning process has been followed correctly it is much easier than just saying, "Well, if we spend five million dollars, we're going to sell a thousand widgets."

Even when objectives are intangible — such as achieving "likability" — KPIs bring some precision into play. If the objective is "We want consumers to like us more", and that is sometimes a relevant objective (an oil company, for example, might want to stop talking about oil and start talking about alternative fuel), the KPIs can be measured against that objective.

While return on investment forecasts will rarely be 100% accurate, they are the first step enabling clients to begin thinking about what return on investment they can get from their communications budgets. Certainly they address the dilemma of a marketing director replying to the boardroom question of "What are we going to get back from all that money you want us to spend on marketing?" If the production director said he wanted to invest $10 million on some new machinery that would improve efficiency by 15%, reduce costs and increase profits, he will get a nod of approval. On the other hand, marketing directors have never really had a credible way of explaining what the company's marcom investment will deliver.

mediaedge:cia

NAVIGATOR™ SUMMARY

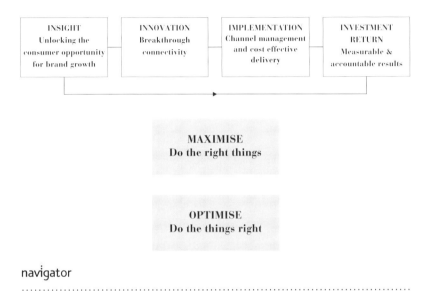

navigator

....

Navigator™ is a real, working model that delivers a unique process for communications planning and implementation. Built into every step are a full suite of proprietary tools and models that add infinitely to the power of the programme. For the sake of confidentiality, these have not been described in this book.

As mentioned earlier, this is not the only channel planning and implementation model available in the market. It is the one of which the authors have an intimate knowledge and a belief that it is at least as effective and advanced as any other. It provides a valuable glimpse into the new approach required from clients if they are to be successful in today's markets. As Jack Klues articulated in *New Yorker*: "The real leaders are the clients who demand more. They recognise that, in the end, the brands that truly distinguish themselves in the market are those that rise above the din of cookie cutter media thinking."

The Navigator™ process is incredibly rigorous and at the same time flexible, in that a client can decide to commission any of the four components in isolation or in any combination.

Because the process is cyclical, it evolves and builds into a culture of ongoing success. It busts old conventions wide open and will no doubt have new challenges of its own to face. But it is all about change as the only constant, and factors that into the process as a constructive force.

The process is based on objectivity and built around unique insights; it encourages creativity at every stage, and invites the best discipline and channel specialists to participate. It also delivers the marketer's Holy Grail: What is my return on investment?

Chapter 11. MOST FREQUENTLY ASKED QUESTIONS

Overall, a brand is a company's ultimate asset. It invests an otherwise generic product or service with a meaning that goes beyond the product itself. Managed correctly, a brand provides some wonderful benefits, not least of which is the ability to charge premium prices; foolishly managed though, it can kill you.
SERGIO ZYMAN

Communications planning and implementation invites many questions — and more than a few challenges. It is new, and because it is based on fundamental change it is likely to make people feel uncomfortable. If it did not, it would not represent real change.

Some of the questions most frequently asked about CP&I are dealt with in this chapter.

"Out of all the marketing services disciplines, why is a media planning and buying specialist best placed to deliver solutions-neutral communications planning and implementation?"

If it is accepted that consumers define brands, and that these days the proliferation of media channels is significantly affecting consumer behaviour, then a broad and deep understanding of the relationship between consumers, the media channels and the brand in question will deliver the key to unlock potential brand growth.

Media specialists are already the leaders when it comes to the inter- and intra-relationships between consumers and media channels. They are also well versed in marketing and brand building.

"In my experience, media people tend to be more administration-based and not necessarily the sort of strategic, innovative or creative people necessary to make CP&I a success — what's changed?"
While this may have been the case in the past, it is changing rapidly. In fact, within those companies that are the leading protagonists of CP&I, the changes started to occur some years ago.

Concerned by the phenomenon of unbundling media from parent agencies, the more visionary ad agency account management professionals are not just sitting it out waiting for extinction. Strong strategists and service executives have already involved themselves within the media specialist community, because that is where they see their future. These days clients will often find that the leading media specialists are increasingly populated by a powerful blend of strategists, account service people, media planners and negotiators from a whole raft of disciplines and backgrounds. They are often brought together in bespoke teams to tackle specific tasks and issues.

"I buy the arguments for CP&I, but doesn't it mean a huge amount of work for my team and I?"
It is fair to say that yes, often there is more work, especially during the first stage of the process, Insight. Long-standing

brand approaches to marketing communications require complete review. Many assumptions and conventions may need to be fundamentally challenged. Often, by the brand owner reviewing and reorganising his activities, significant efficiencies and quite possibly, cost synergies will result. Improved value and organisation from research is a frequent outcome. Generally, research is disjointed and managed by a number of different departments within client organisations. Research projects are undertaken on new product development (NPD), separate from sales data, separate from brand health checks, separate again from communications studies. These four different types of research projects can all be of huge value to communications planning simply through sensible coordination and by adding some appropriate "when" and "where" type questions.

The media specialist undertakes the vast majority of the project management and coordination work in collaboration with the client and discipline specialists, always checking and challenging through an ongoing process of dialogue.

Once the work is done however, the client and media specialist will have achieved the freedom to look objectively at all potential discipline and channel mixes. In one sense, it could be argued that this is work that clients cannot afford *not* to do. All too commonly millions of dollars in marketing funds are allocated and spent on flawed premises, a scenario that more often than not is disastrous.

"As a brand marketer, isn't CP&I what I'm supposed to be doing?"

As recently as five years ago the answer would probably have been yes. Today however the ever-increasing array of marketing disciplines (and, within them, the available channels that have become enormously specialised) makes it an almost impossible task for a marketer to accomplish on his own.

People from marketing services backgrounds often forget the massive challenges facing today's marketers. The functions and tasks go way beyond just planning and implementing marketing communications programmes. For example, marketers need to be constantly reviewing their product features and benefits against competitors, managing relationships with distributors and retailers, and devising product offers that make sense commercially to both the trade and consumers. They have to review the implications of the supply chain on product availability and delivery times, and work closely with research and new product development teams to ensure that new products will gain a commercial franchise in the marketplace. The list is endless. It is just not realistic to expect marketers to also be communications planners and implementers in this day of information overload and immense specialisation.

"Why do I need CP&I?"

Simply because it is the surest way to achieve organic growth through investment in marketing communications. While nobody denies that growth may be achieved by going directly to any of the specialist marketing disciplines, an objectively planned and managed investment synchronised across the *full* gamut of disciplines and channels is more likely to deliver planned growth and accountability.

Marketers need to ask themselves the following 10 questions and reply with brutal honesty. If the answer to any of them is negative, then their brand could benefit from CP&I:

1. Do we have clear, measurable and achievable objectives for brand growth?
2. Have these been clearly communicated to, and accepted by, our marketing services partners?
3. Have we really taken a holistic approach to brand communications planning and thoroughly evaluated our brand — in the context of the market, the channels, consumer behaviour and the competition?
4. Do we really know our consumers, their likes and dislikes, their attitudes and values, and how they interact with our brands?
5. Do we have a full understanding of how our consumers are influenced by the media channels and how our brand can best interact with the consumer in that context?
6. Have we taken a holistic approach to innovation and creativity — through considering how we connect our brand to the consumers in a genuinely solutions-neutral environment?
7. Have we done due diligence on the allocation of our budgets across channels and our expectations for our investment return?
8. Have we shared **all** our relevant knowledge, information

and research with our marketing services partners?

9. Do our current marketing services partners from each specialised discipline currently work as an integrated team with the common objective of growing our brand?

10. Are we comfortable that our marketing service partners are being sensibly remunerated for their services and that they are motivated towards our success through incentives for measurable growth?

"To work with CP&I, will I need to give away a raft of proprietary and confidential information — and how can I feel secure in sharing this?"

Regardless of the way you choose to manage your external marketing partners, sharing confidential information should already be the case. If it is not, then it will be extremely difficult for them to provide you with the insightful work necessary for success.

For clients to enjoy total confidentiality, total trust is essential. And to have any chance of achieving total trust, there has to be a very clear understanding of expectations on both sides. That trust is founded on a fair remuneration policy that allows the external marketing partner to do what they are in business to do — make a profit in return for the valuable work they provide. In other words, win, win. If that is the case, then a client can expect and more often than not receive, not only total confidentiality, but also the best brains, resources and effectively preferred client status.

If on the other hand the client has successfully negotiated all the margin out of his partner's remuneration, then why on earth should he expect any trust and loyalty? In all likelihood his account is being used short-term to build a knowledge set that will one day be instrumental in winning a competitor's business who *is* prepared to remunerate his partner with a fair profit margin.

In this scenario, not only is the client likely to have the weaker brains and talent allocated to his business, but his account team will be out in the marketplace selling their experience and knowledge gained from working on his unprofitable business. Lose, lose.

"How much will CP&I cost, how will it be charged, and how will the value compare with my existing arrangements?"
By definition, CP&I must be charged on a time cost basis. In fact, it is difficult to see how CP&I could be delivered successfully if it is compensated on a commission basis. If commissionable channels are the key drivers, then the solutions will invariably be the conventional advertising routes of TV, print and so on. The absolute cost will depend entirely on the size and scope of the project, which obviously can vary enormously.

"Won't CP&I fundamentally change the way that we manage our marketing communications suppliers — isn't it all too difficult?"
Growth is every marketer's objective and responsibility. It is a universal truth that change is the only constant. As such, one has to recognise, accept and act upon the fundamentally changed circumstances that now affect brands, consumers, and their interaction with media channels. If it is too difficult

to manage now, it will become increasingly more difficult the longer the status quo remains.

"Can small and medium advertisers 'afford' CP&I?"
The reality for small- and medium-sized marketers is that if the small want to become medium-sized, and the medium-sized want to become large, then they cannot afford *not* to embrace CP&I. One of the benefits of CP&I is that it is flexible and rigorous. Clients can buy part of the process, or the full process, depending on their needs and budgets. **The issues are brand growth and visibility, not money.**

Why should clients with smaller budgets be invisible? Instead of an average-sized budget getting an average advertising solution, channel planning can help them break out of the vicious circle of disconnectivity between their brand, their consumers and the communications channels to achieve significantly better returns on investment.

In fact, smaller- to medium-sized clients are often more open to channel planning. They recognise that they have to be more innovative and different in the way they use their marketing funds in order to compete effectively with the larger players in the market.

Naturally enough, **the great temptation for most clients who feel they have a tight budget will be to spend everything on exposure**. Given a choice, they will often forsake an insight-based approach to innovation and stake their future on a mediocre execution that gets lots of exposure for whatever budget they have. Just pick up a daily newspaper or watch a couple of commercial breaks on TV to see the proof.

A smarter course would be to take a small portion of their budget, say 10%, and invest that in gaining real insights that unlock a deeper understanding of how their consumers behave, how their consumers connect with the media, and connect with the brand. Armed with those insights, they could build a channel planning strategy so that every single dollar they spend does the work of three or four.

Medium-sized advertisers are often concerned that their smaller budgets will not allow them to shout as loud as their bigger competitors. Yet, as we have seen, **shouting is not the issue**. Even with the major advertisers, there is an increasing view that marketing communications are conversations between brands and consumers through the media, and with conversations we talk — not shout. Even the bigger brands need to be far smarter, because increasingly they get into the territory where by shouting too loudly, they become irritating and create negativity. The last thing a medium-sized client needs is "loudness". His first priority should be maximising his return on investment.

"How should retail advertisers use channel planning and implementation?"

Retail advertising is bound by many conventions. Suppliers fund much of it. As a result, retail print ads are universally crammed with supplier merchandise. The opportunity to build the retailer's own brand and position the store as a community of trust is lost. Retail advertising can work hard in sales terms while building a retail brand with the same money. (And if suppliers are paying for it, so much the better!)

Generally, retailers are resistant to planning. They perceive it as a "cost" when actually the reverse is true. CP&I will help retailers secure even greater return on investment by providing actionable insights into their category and their target audience. If their consumers confessed they were interested to discover new things, to buy new things, and be seen in the "right" kind of retail environment, then the last thing that would attract them is a double-page spread full of prices. If a retailer invested in holistic planning, the consumer insight could well be "I want to have a great shopping experience". Then his priority would be to brush up the shopping experience he offered and make it consistent across all his stores before he even thought about advertising.

There is no denying that thousands of women go through the minutiae of the newspaper ads looking for bargains. Yet a considerable proportion of the market will buy by association. Waitrose in the UK, for example, might run a double-page spread in all the upmarket magazines showing a fishing boat in a beautiful loch in Scotland. Somewhere in that huge, compelling shot will be a line of type that says something to the effect of "Scottish salmon, £2.99 a pound." The message that comes through is that Waitrose is all about quality, and good prices, but very much in that order. It leaves the consumer with the impression that they have a fantastic product, and it implies that everything else sold in Waitrose is of the same standard.

In Asia, IKEA has pointed the way. It does a terrific job in selling merchandise and building its brand because it creates interest in the product and de-commoditises it, while its competitors commoditise everything. Admittedly,

Building interest in IKEA. A little dog does not recognise his home because his owners have shopped at IKEA. Lowe & Partners Singapore.

IKEA is different in that IKEA sells only IKEA products; it is both the manufacturer and the retailer. Therefore every element of IKEA is IKEA; it is the brand in every sense. These days however, most leading retailers have their own "house" brands, but largely they sell other people's brands and their advertising is funded by their suppliers who want to see their products. Unfortunately in Asia, retailers allow the trading aspect of their business to dictate how they communicate their business — as opposed to deciding **strategically** how they want to communicate their business.

"How can communications channel planning be really solutions-neutral when its practitioners still earn a considerable proportion of their revenues from conventional media planning and buying?"

It is true to say that all media specialists continue to earn a considerable proportion of their revenues from selling their media planning and buying services. For those that have a genuine CP&I offer, the proportions are shifting at a rapid pace.

The insight and experience gained from strategic media planning and buying is a key to the development of the CP&I offer. In a number of ways, it is the inter- and intra-relationships between the consumer and the media channels that are at the heart of the CP&I process. And strategic media planning and buying is in fact part of the CP&I process under the third "I", Implementation.

To achieve commercial success, those companies offering CP&I services will need to sell them as an additional service to existing clients, based on a time cost remuneration model totally separate to any other arrangements that may exist for other media services. The same will be true when selling the service to new clients. By selling the CP&I service on a time cost basis, any possible conflict of interest is effectively removed.

In all likelihood, media specialists will continue to earn significant revenues from strategic media planning and buying, but the proportions will shift in favour of revenue from their CP&I services.

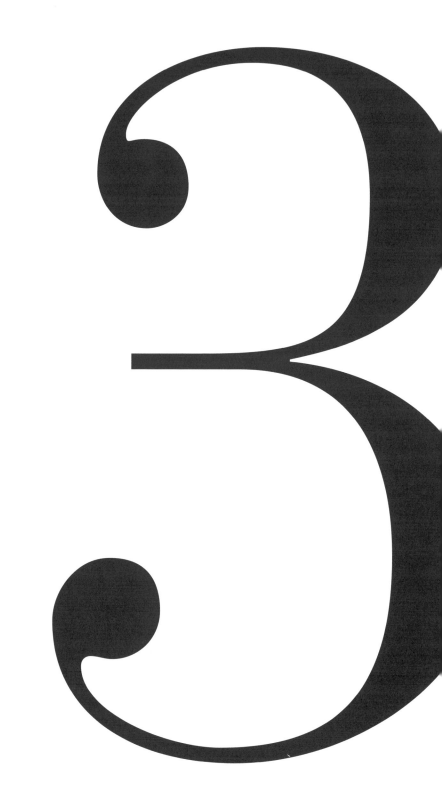

BRAVE
NEW
WORLD

Chapter 12

REWRITING THE RULES

Over the next 40 years, as always, there will be winners and losers. The winners will be those who continue to combine an informed and intuitive sense of business with an alchemist's ability to turn strategy into enviable execution. These are the companies that will make their clients successful, earn themselves authority and thereby fully justify their premium price. The losers will be those who turn their backs on the business of business in the sole pursuit of some unanchored concept called creativity.
JEREMY BULLMORE

The new twenty-first century marketing communications business will not use the word "agency" in its description. ("Any business with the word agency in its title is dead," confirms Nicholas Negroponte, Media Lab guru at the Massachusetts Institute of Technology.)

Nor is it likely to house a creative department.

And nor will it earn its revenues from traditional media commissions.

What else is on the cards?

Perhaps clients will form their own conglomerates to deliver their own marketing services needs. This has happened in the Netherlands, and is happening in Taiwan.

Possibly, they will form partnerships and joint ventures with marketing services companies based on the Japanese "partnership sourcing" model which will be discussed in this chapter.

Certainly, the new marketing communications industry will see clients paying for everything as they ask for it, very likely from a pre-defined rate card. Everything will be transparent. And profits will be largely dependent upon the results achieved for the clients.

Managing An Agency Partner: Are Agencies Overpaid Or Underpaid For Their Services?

Why does considerable distrust exist between marketers and their advertising agencies? Some point to the commission system and the non-transparent agency income levels like markups on production and other third-party costs.

But while clients often feel that agencies abuse them, agencies feel the reverse is true. Clients abuse their time — the only thing they have to sell. And in some markets, media commissions are again an issue: agencies would argue that clients should not expect transparency especially when they sometimes demand commission rates as low as 1%!

Before genuine transparency can be achieved, much more open, honest discussion is required along with trust and mutual respect. When clients are asked by agencies, "Do you care if your business is profitable to us?", more often than not the answer is either directly, or indirectly, "No, I don't care". Which begs the question, what do these clients expect the agency to do — run their account at a loss for a short period of time and then relinquish it, or reduce the quality of service so they get what they actually pay for? In other words, do some clients think that it is sustainable or sensible for an agency to effectively subsidise their marketing investments? Agencies, after all, are in business to make a profit, too.

To be fair, the marketing services industry is equally at fault. Highly competitive new business pitches, where agency reputations are on the line, often drive agencies to win at any cost, and that cost often means "buying" new accounts at a loss.

Marketers should probe whether their business is profitable to their agency and regularly monitor the situation through in-depth reviews of the service delivery and corresponding agency remuneration. If a marketer's business is profitable to an agency then he has every right to expect very strong, consistent service delivered by the agency's most talented teams. If he does not get it, he has every right to complain and consider putting his business up for competitive review. (In Asia, of course, as a result of global agency alignments, there is little some marketers can do about the quality of service they receive.)

In the Asian context, given the climate of uncertainty, many agencies and marketing services companies live in a constant state of low-level fear that if they put one foot wrong their clients will fire them. The argument frequently heard is that it is better not to hold a relationship review with a client: it might give the client the idea of holding a competitive review instead. All in all, it is an unhealthy state of affairs when the agency-client relationship is supposedly based on partnership.

Once, agency-client relationships were about a genuine partnership. Clients really believed that agencies did build their brands for them. And while some clients still believe that a partnership approach is more productive, many more don't want one — **they want a client-supplier relationship**. Every dollar they can squeeze from suppliers goes onto their bottom line. In turn, this short-term approach causes many problems with the output from agencies, problems with creative consistency, commitment, quality and innovation. If brand owners did make sure that their business was profitable to their agency partners, agencies would get better at what they do. Agencies could reinvest more of their profits in training, attract better talent into the business, and then the whole industry would become more professional. At present, many agencies are profitable only because their staff is prepared to work all hours for their clients. If their staff were to work to rule — eight hours a day, five days a week — one would probably see pretty well every agency in Asia out of business within six months. While it has become somewhat of a cliché, it is also a fundamental truth for agencies to say their only real asset is people.

If a client does *not care* whether his account is profitable to his partners, or if he is deliberately forcing the agency to run his account at a loss, he is encouraging agencies and other marketing services companies to supplement their incomes in nontransparent ways. He is not only perpetuating a cycle of nontransparent earnings, poor quality service and constant conflict in the relationship. He is contributing to the decline of an industry that is still intrinsically important to him, and frankly an industry which people are leaving in their hundreds. Stress is the major factor. In fact, few talented young Asians go into advertising; they go into banking, or shipping, or manufacturing, or information technology. Advertising is seen as a low-paid, low-face industry. There is not even much glamour left to compensate for the hours of sweat and frustration.

Planning: In The Wrong Place?

Account planning, the panacea of marketing communications pioneered by British advertising agency Boase Massimi Pollitt, is a discipline designed to explore the consumer's relationship with the brand. By getting under the skin of both the brand and the consumer, planners can understand how they will fit together and how the creative advertising should best present the brand to the consumer.

One of the world's foremost account planners, Jon Steel, defines the planner's job as "providing the key decision makers at both the agency and the client with all the information they require to make an intelligent decision". Steel argues that a planner's aim is "the production of the best possible advertising to fulfil the client's business objectives, advertising that will stand out from the crowd, say the right things to the right people, and cause them to take some action as a result of seeing or hearing the message. It's that little reaction in their heads that the planner is seeking." His book, *Truth, Lies & Advertising*, presents many outstanding case histories where the planner's detective work provided fresh insights that led to strategic and creative breakthroughs.

The great British planning guru Leslie Butterfield called a planner "the representative of the consumer within the agency".

Well and good, but account planning only works when a client is willing to pay for it — and an agency commits to offering it in its proper form. And even then, the function needs to be considered within the context of the new dynamic. It must take into account the effects of the contact points.

the content and the context to deliver genuinely valuable connections with consumers.

If an account planner is really supposed to be the architect of how the brand connects with the consumer, why does the connection always have to be an "ad"?

Arguably, account planning presently is a department of an advertising agency whose *raison d'être* is to produce great advertising, not to produce great solutions-neutral marketing communications plans. In many quarters, account planning is the subject of controversy. Cynics argue that great creative and account service people have always performed the planning function anyhow, albeit intuitively. Then there is the argument that account planning is actually the post-rationalisation department for the creative agency's output of TV commercials and double-page spreads.

Some suggest it isn't that the function of planning is wrong, but question whether it is in the right place. **To achieve the discipline's full potential, they argue, shouldn't the account planner sit above an ad agency — in a completely solutions-neutral environment?** Their point is that he should work with a choice of different communications agencies around him, so he can take the best options for a brand — only *one* of which might be advertising — and mix them. Given the new dynamic, all the massive changes in communications, and the fact that the absolute number and combinations of choices have grown exponentially in the last five years and will double again in the next two — and not forgetting the impending explosion in digital communications — their argument gains credence.

In fact, over four years ago Rob Norman, CEO of Outrider, the digital arm of Mediaedge:cia, predicted the emergence of the **superplanner** — a function combining the skills of the media planner and the account planner. This individual would interface between clients, agencies, and the channels. According to Norman, superplanners "will own the channel strategy that they will develop in cooperation with the client and his other agency resources, born out of a deep understanding of the consumer. Their job will be to understand the communications objectives and strategy, and to find the appropriate range of channels to deliver that strategy." They will have to understand environment, consumer behaviour, competitive behaviour, and the accumulated effect of all the proposed activity on the client's business.

The concept of a superplanner offers a compelling "what if" scenario as we look at the future construct of the advertising agency.

How Will Advertising Agencies Reinvent Themselves?
Unilever chairman Niall FitzGerald said, "I do not find today's advertising agencies much of a match for tomorrow's market opportunities."

Agencies have to redefine their value to brand owners by totally restructuring their business model.

And brand owners, for their own good, must be open to encouraging and helping their agencies take the radical steps necessary to restructure their businesses. They cannot on the one hand demand change, and then on the other withdraw from taking the risks always associated with the very change they have mandated. Significantly, on the client side, Unilever is leading the way.

For decades, the fundamental construct of advertising agencies was built around departments of artists and writers, cloistered away behind the commercial people, and supported by the administratively-led media department. In the context of the new dynamic, and given the unbundling of media departments, the question is: where should we go from here?

Three "what if" scenarios for the future:

1. Unbundling the creative department

At present most, if not all agencies claim the quality of their creative output as their point of difference against their competition. Their main selling point is, "We make a difference through our creative". To have any chance of delivering this, they have to have the best people (for best read "most expensive") populating their creative departments. By necessity they seek out the high profile work, which is TV or large print work, and too often creativity in agencies is just about the message or content. Creative departments are highly volatile environments, and the commercial and opportunity costs of operating these creative machines are huge. Agency managers are caught in a real trap. How can they deliver a point of difference (meaning how can they be the most creative), yet at the same time be totally neutral in terms of the right solution? It seems an impossible dilemma.

The key issue that has to be tackled by global ad agency management teams is how should the expensive yet critical creative talent be organised in a way that will ensure relevance to clients and achieve ongoing

commercial success?

One solution which requires guts, determination and a belief in the future, is to set up the creative department as a separate independent business — performing in its own commercially accountable way.

It would no longer be enshrined behind an account service department whose job it was to be sales agents for the creatives. The creative department would go the way of the media department: it would become an independent business in its own right. And like the media independents, it would need to sustain profitable growth. It would be paid on results and no longer be able to languish as an ongoing fixed cost, paid regardless of client demand or the quality of its work. But through its involvement as a key part of the channel planning and implementation process, the creative independent would be better placed to deliver the right solutions to clients with creativity based on a far broader definition and spanning all possible routes to connect with the consumer. As Jeremy Bullmore so eloquently articulated at the beginning of this chapter, it would have a fighting chance of achieving the ultimate: "An alchemist's ability to turn strategy into enviable execution."

Heresy? Bill Bernbach changed the face of advertising 40 years ago in a very different world. What would he do today? The dynamics that existed in his day are no longer there, and it is simply impossible to make a difference just through creative. From what we know of Bernbach, he responded to the dynamics around him. He might well agree that in today's context, having great creativity *per se* is neither a strategy nor a solution in itself.

2. New marketing communications business models would evolve, based on the merger of account planning and strategic media planning

Assuming the agency is left without its creative and media wings, who remains and what do they do?

Today, without control of the media function, agency account management teams are hard pressed to concretely define the added value they bring to a client's business. Take the creative function away and it would become impossible. As we have seen earlier, the demise in importance of the account management function is due to circumstance not ability. Some of the most talented "suits" have already found that their natural home in the future lies with those media specialists leading the field in the development and delivery of channel planning and implementation. A similar transition would be relatively straightforward for account planners. In the CP&I environment, talented planners would have the freedom to seek solutions that were not of necessity pre-defined as ads.

In this scenario, the service sitting at the head of the client's table will be based upon communications planning and implementation. In some ways, we may see the clock turned back to the days when great senior "suits" in agencies formulated great strategies, when men like Maurice Saatchi, Tim Bell, Frank Lowe and Ian Batey contributed brilliant thinking that led to brilliant creative executions, long before the days of the planner. They would be perceived in much the same light as the most talented conductors of the greatest orchestras.

This lends itself to the merger of the account planning

and strategic media planning functions to combine into a new breed of superplanner, powerfully armed with the communications planning and implementation process.

And as an outcome, **a new specialist skill will emerge: the communications implementer, or project manager, a complementary role to the communications channel planner.** These individuals will have the talent to manage and implement the increasingly complex communications planning process for clients. In today's world, there are two sets of people who appear best placed to claim this role. The first are brand managers currently sitting within client companies: their historic experience in orchestrating the different facets of marketing communications lends itself naturally to this new function. The second are the stronger account managers from the best agencies who long for the opportunity to once again deliver real value to their client's marketing activity. As communications project managers they would achieve that ambition, and reinvent themselves with purpose and credibility.

Already, a new breed of agency is emerging across the world, challenging and disrupting convention: CIA's Nota Bene in South Africa, Singapore's Red Card, the UK's Naked, Australia's Bellamy & Hayden, and Fusion 5 in the US. Different, Big Fat, Maverick and Assassination are others. Admittedly they tend to be localised.

Meanwhile some of the larger media specialists are well down the road to achieving an ambitious goal: becoming the first true global practitioners of insightful and accountable communications planning and implementation.

3. Media commissions will be abolished. The client will pay for everything — or nothing. And everything will have to be transparent

Clients will pay for communications channel planning advice and all the potential facets of its implementation.

If media owners no longer paid commissions, the likely outcome is that advertising agencies and media specialists would have to say to their clients, "Now that I don't get paid by a third-party supplier (the media owner), I need to talk to you about *you* paying me." And the clients would either have to say, "Yes, I do value your services so I am prepared to pay you an agreed fee for your time," or "No, I'm not going to pay you. I'll hire someone else or do it myself." The abolition of media commissions would create massive short-term turmoil for the industry, but it would, once and for all, flush the industry out and would at last help turn it from an "industry" into a "profession".

It would force clients to start paying for what they actually valued, and eradicate the ambiguity and lack of clarity that surround the existing remuneration structure. It would have the potential to bring the whole basis of remuneration above the line.

Will We See Virtual Agencies?

The world's first global creative independent was launched in December 2002 and operates borderlessly on the Web. Its business model offers through-the-line creativity to marketers, design companies, media specialists, management consultancies — and other advertising agencies.

It was launched by a major mainstream agency with

a strong through-the-line tradition to deliver **"integrated communications that transcend advertising solutions"**.

Called The Dukes of Urbino.Com, its primary creative and strategic service provider is The Jupiter Drawing Room, South Africa, recently ranked one of the top five most creative agencies in the world by US trade publication *Advertising Age Creativity*. Its clients include Nike, Fiat and The Coca-Cola Company. "We believe the time is right for an initiative of this nature," said Graham Warsop, founder of The Jupiter Drawing Room. "Certain critical factors have come together at a unique moment in the history of our industry." Warsop said that the advancement of technology such as video conferencing and the Web were key factors in making the new model viable.

Not only will The Dukes of Urbino.Com work for any brand owner in any country, it will also source creative input from an international pool of talent.

Will "Partnership Sourcing" Create A New Kind Of Agency-Client Relationship?

Long ago the Japanese developed the concept of partnership sourcing for the automotive industry. It was one of the reasons why the Japanese car industry became world-beating in the 1980s and 1990s. The proposition was simple: in the relationship between manufacturer and supplier (read "client and agency"), both parties committed to do whatever they reasonably could to improve the profitability, quality and efficiency of each other's operations. Utopia, or laughable?

If the relationships between the marketing services community and its clients were similarly re-engineered, the industry and its clients would have a strong chance of growth through mutual success. It would self-perpetuate trust, innovation, security and accountability. It would lead to a virtuous, symbiotic circle of growth. (There are already signs of this happening, such as the deal struck between Dentsu and Sony in Japan last year. Dentsu bought a large stake in one of Sony's in-house agencies in return for securing Sony's media advertising and content development across Asia.)

Will Clients Start Their Own Agencies?

It has happened in the past and it could happen again — perhaps under a slightly different guise. Some would argue that even if only a quarter of the issues raised in this chapter eventuated, they would be left with no choice.

Many clients have established their own in-house departments producing catalogues, point-of-sale materials and print. Their business model is inevitably based on efficiencies and the savings made by dispensing with external suppliers like agencies and design houses. And yes, the savings on third-party profit margins do offset the new overheads they incur. And yes, they can even make a notional profit into the bargain. The only stumbling block is talent. They cannot attract, motivate and keep the great strategists and creative talent to drive their business. So eventually they have to outsource. Back to square one.

In concert with the right, rigorous process, it is always the really great people from all disciplines that make the crucial difference.

Will Clients Start Communications Conglomerates Of Their Own?

This is an important question and one that needs to be answered. Certainly such a development would not be within the existing core competency of client companies. However, as an increasing number of global blue-chip companies state that their long term ambition is to outsource everything — including manufacturing — and effectively become marketing companies, it is not that much of a leap of the imagination to see them considering insourcing much of the marketing function that is currently outsourced.

Marketers have also demonstrated their ability to form their own alliances with media owners. Procter & Gamble signed a US$300 million global cross-media deal with Viacom. According to the *Financial Times* on 23 April 2002, "As much as 40% of P&G's total media budget could eventually be locked up in this kind of deal with the world's biggest media companies."

One outcome of the global consolidation of marketing services over the past decade is that clients are faced with fewer and fewer choices. Some undoubtedly could decide to consider alternative solutions — such as forming themselves into something similar to the Korean *chaebol* model to deliver their marketing communications services. (Samsung, for example, owns Korea's largest ad agency, the mammoth Cheil Communications.)

However such a development would require "co-opetition", which in the past has proven spectacularly difficult to achieve successfully.

Will Agencies Be Paid On Results?

The Incorporated Society of British Advertisers estimates that 50% of major advertisers now have some element of payment by results (PBR) in their agency remuneration packages. And it is the clients who are pushing for more of it. As one advertiser argues, "We sink or swim together."

Risk and Reward (R&R) income is the manifestation of payment by results at UK agency TBWA. According to the *Financial Times*, 13 August 2002, the agency will now receive 40p for every hectolitre (176 pints) of lager that Holsten Pils sells. The agency will receive no other payment for its day-to-day work on the client's business.

TBWA UK's then chief executive Garry Lace believed the traditional agency business model was flawed. "The models that have been used in the past, commission (15% of the total budget) and fixed fees, don't actually reward agencies for what they bring to clients — ideas that drive commercial success."

On the client side, Holsten marketing chief Andy Edge had been looking for a more equal way of sharing both the risks and rewards. "If an advertising campaign under-performed," he said, "there was no downside for the agency in terms of what it would be paid."

But what about factors beyond the agency's control? For instance, what happens if poor weather dampens drinkers' thirsts, or sales are hit by a rival price promotion? As Lace put it, "They're issues the client has to deal with, so why not the agency?"

Air Miles and Virgin One are other clients that pay TBWA based on a single measure of performance. Air Miles paid the agency for every Sainsbury's Reward Cardholder converted to Tesco, Air Miles' new partner. Financial services brand Virgin One pays TBWA for every initial contact it receives from potential customers.

TBWA is so committed to R&R income that it wants 50% of its revenues based on some form of PBR within three years.

What Will Happen When Media Is Bought On-line? Commoditisation?

The sooner the agency commission system is abolished, the better. One factor that might act as a catalyst is when all media is bought on-line and the costs of service are based on a cost-per-transaction model.

At one time WPP, Omnicom and Interpublic formed a working party to explore how they could create an on-line buying system. Were media to be bought on-line, vast media-buying empires would be aligned to do business with vast media-owning empires. On an operational level, one bank of computers would interact with another bank of computers to dramatically reduce the cost of providing many elements of the media buying process. For those aspects of the business that are commoditised, it will all be about the lowest cost of doing business. These new media trading monoliths would charge clients on a cost-per-transaction basis in much the same way that stockbrokers charge their clients. For example, an on-line stockbroking company might charge, say, $20 per transaction, whether a client is buying a million dollars' worth of shares or a hundred dollars' worth, because the cost of executing the transaction is $16 and their aim is to make a 20% profit margin.

When media trading is all done on-line, that will kill commissions. There will be no justification for anyone to receive a commission. But this new breed of media buying company will still make money because the cost of doing business will be that much cheaper. They will dramatically reduce staff levels and have computers working 24 hours a day, seven days a week. It is a logical progression. All companies, in every business sector, are looking at how they can reduce the cost of doing business. For a number of years technology has enabled computers to have relationships as buyers and sellers. Computers could process hundreds of thousands of transactions an hour, doing the work of manual media buyers in minutes rather than hours or days.

Of course media owners will still require their sales departments, albeit smaller ones, that will sell to those who control the relevant implementation budgets. Negotiations on price will be conducted as they are now, with the "added value" element of the negotiation agreed at the outset. Once the deal is struck, it would go into the system and the computers would take over.

WHATEVER happens, one fact will remain. Marketing communications will always be about **conversations** between brands and consumers. And for any conversation to be successful, it needs to be a mutually valuable exchange of ideas and information where both parties are actively listening to the other without wasting precious time and attention. And yes, there will always be somebody out there. And because we will understand them better, and understand their relationships with brands and channels better, successful marketing communications will talk to them with simplicity, relevance and respect.

APPENDIX

A week before this book went to press, The Coca-Cola Company's President and Chief Operating Officer Steven Heyer delivered a landmark speech at *Advertising Age's* first Madison + Vine conference at the Beverly Hills Hotel, Los Angeles, on 5 February 2003.

Heyer challenged marketers, media and agency heads to rethink the assumptions behind their present business models.

Extracts of his speech demonstrate Heyer's vision that marketing must be re-engineered and how Coca-Cola will be a world leader in the new reality:

"At The Coca-Cola Company we're thinking about marketing in a radically different way. And I'd suggest that those of you here today who aren't yet thinking this way ought to start right now.

Economic and social developments demand a new approach to connecting with audiences, with consumers:

- The economic landscape around media cost efficiencies
- The escalation of property and sponsorship costs
- The trifecta that is fragmentation and proliferation of media, and the consolidation of media ownership — soon to be followed by a wholesale unbundling
- The erosion of mass markets
- The empowerment of consumers who now have an unrivalled ability to edit and avoid advertising and to shift day parts

- A consumer trend toward mass customisation and personalisation
- And the emergence of an experience-based economy, where cultural production is more important than physical production.

I am describing a magnitude and urgency of change that isn't evolutionary — it's transformational. And as leaders in consumer packaged goods, Coca-Cola will go first.

Where will Coke go? To accelerate the convergence of Madison & Vine — a convergence of the trinity in brand building — content, and media, and marketing.

This is a convergence born of necessity. Economic necessity and marketplace opportunity. We need each other — now more than ever. We need each other to capture people's attention and influence their attitudes and behaviours…

So how does Madison meet Vine? What's the intersection?

It's not the property, the TV show, the movie, the music or the brand. **It's about why, where and how we bring them together. And it is, as ever, about the consumer, all glued together by a powerful idea.**

It's the insight about people's passions and the connections we create — naturally and uniquely — between them and the equity in our brands. Cultural icons in brand context. Important events tied to important brands… with an important reason why…

We must create more value for consumers, audiences, and customers… through cooperation, collaboration, and innovation in marketing and communication… Through working together to create something for our brands that matters more on Main Street and ultimately on Wall Street. For The Coca-Cola Company, that's value around the bottle that's at least as great as the value in the bottle.

Because creating value around this bottle is the secret formula of Coca-Cola's success. Coca-Cola isn't black water with a little sugar and a lot of fizz… Coca-Cola isn't a drink. It's an idea. Like great movies, like great music, Coca-Cola is a feeling.

Coca-Cola is refreshment and connection. Always has been…always will be. That's a timeless proposition. But we express it in the unique vocabulary of each generation, for what's timeless must also be timely — or it's dated…

But that's no longer enough. So where are we going?

Away from spots in pods.

Away from broadcast TV as the anchor medium.

Away from product placements that are gratuitous because they lack a compelling idea. Because in today's marketing and media environment only the naïve and foolish confuse presence with impact. "Presence is easy — impact is hard."

Away from discrete media elements of any and all types.

Away from traditional relationships with agencies, the Hollywood community, the sports community and many of our customers.

So where are we headed? We're headed to ideas. Not properties *per se*, but intellectual property. Ideas that bring entertainment value to our brands, and ideas that integrate our brands into entertainment…

We will use a diverse array of entertainment assets to break into people's hearts and minds. In that order. For this is the way to their wallets. Always has been. Always will be. This much hasn't changed. We're moving to ideas that elicit emotion and create connections.

Markets are giving way to networks. In a networked economy, ideas, concepts, and images are the items of real value…

So do we need reach and frequency — no. We need idea driven connection with our targets. Our marketing efforts, our properties and media and celebrity deals will only produce an adequate return on investment if we use our network of bottlers, customers, promotional partners, properties and associations to add value beyond the bottle and enrich the lives of our consumers…

People are always saying that this medium or that medium is in decay, declining, going away. No medium goes away; its role changes. That's all. **And as media fragmentation continues…and as new choices continue to emerge and technology leaps out ahead of consumers' wishes to change the way they behave…it's incumbent upon us all — advertisers, marketers, creators of content and culture, everyone in this game — to think. And to think differently about how we'll connect with consumers in the future…**

And I'd like to suggest that we think about using any and all media in a new way. It's something we can all access. The concept is simple: create value for people…

that lives beyond and extends the immediate moment of consumption... connecting with their passions... enriched experiences that drive brand strength and product sales.

How? By aggregating our properties in a network of touch points that enrich people's lives. Experience-based, access-driven marketing is our next frontier.

As we move to an experience-based economy, the effective use of relevant and powerful cultural references takes a front seat. Each person's life becomes a commercial market. And any ad agency that thinks a jingle connects like real music, or a powerful movie, and doesn't collaborate, is lost.

Imagine if we used our collective toolkit to create an ever-expanding variety of interactions for people that — over time — built a relationship, an on-going series of transactions, that is unique, differentiated and deeper... improving everyone's economics and reversing the buyer-seller, zero-sum game.

Managing the quality of our consumer relationships — together — should take on the same urgency that controlling the means of production once did... Powerful expression of ideas, not hard assets.

In this new marketing world we need to look at one another not in terms of how much we can pay, but in terms of what we can do and make together. How we can exchange value to create value...

We're all comfortable with our traditional roles.

Hollywood creates culture, defines what's interesting, hip and relevant. Madison Avenue interprets brand values and defines the connections to culture in a contemporary and interesting way. Marketers build programmes that glue together a multiplicity of relationships to create the reasons why we are entitled to a consumer's loyalty and a premium price.

Those clear-cut definitions fit neatly into a box... a box defined by uniformity and predictability, which is no longer sustainable in a hyper-fragmenting world. If we continue to confine ourselves to those roles, that box is going to become a coffin. The headstone will read: 'They didn't try'.

We don't intend to get buried. I don't think you do either. So each of us needs to think outside that box. **We need to broaden the definition of our roles. We need to leverage a powerful network held together by an unseen fabric of connections.**

All of us in the game... those who make television shows, video games, music and movies... those who build brands... and those who help connect those brands with consumers through the elements of popular culture need to establish enhanced relationships with one another in an effort to deliver unique experiences to the consumer.

That's a new model for a new era. 'An era of co-creation.' It is what The Coca-Cola Company will insist on from its partners. But it isn't something The Coca-Cola Company can build alone. It's a model we need to build together... at the intersection of Madison and Vine.

We just put a big sign in the window — 'Partners Wanted'. The Coca-Cola Company is open for business."

To view the full speech, please visit www.AdAdge.com

IBLIOGRAPHY

Aitchison, Jim.
Cutting Edge Advertising.
Prentice Hall, 1999.

Bond, Jonathan and Kirshenbaum, Richard.
Under the Radar: Talking to Today's Cynical Consumer.
John Wiley & Sons, 1998.

British Design & Art Direction.
Rewind: Forty Years of Design and Advertising.
Phaidon Press, 2002.

Dru, Jean-Marie.
Beyond Disruption: Changing the Rules in the Marketplace.
John Wiley & Sons, 2002.

Ehrenberg, A. S. C.
Repetitive Advertising and the Consumer.
Journal of Advertising Research, April 1979.

Ehrenberg, A. S. C., Barnard, Neil and Scriven, John.
Advertising is Publicity Not Persuasion.
South Bank University, London, 1998.

Festinger, Leon.
A Theory of Cognitive Dissonance.
Row, Peterson, 1957.

Gladwell, Malcolm.
The Tipping Point: How Little Things Can Make a Big Difference.
Little, Brown & Company, 2000.

Klein, Naomi.
No Logo.
Flamingo, 2000.

Krugman, Herbert E.
The Impact of Television Advertising: Learning without Involvement.
Public Opinion Quarterly, Vol. XXIX, No. 3, Fall 1965.

Levine, Rick, Locke, Christopher, Searls, Doc and Weinberger, David.
The Cluetrain Manifesto: The End of Business As Usual.
Perseus Publishing, 2000.

Mackay, Hugh.
The Good Listener.
Pan Macmillan Australia, 1998.

Monbiot, George.
Captive State.
Macmillan, 2000.

Sacharin, Ken.
Attention! How to Interrupt, Yell, Whisper, and Touch Consumers.
John Wiley & Sons, 2001.

Schlosser, Eric.
Fast Food Nation.
Houghton, 2000.

Steel, Jon.
Truth, Lies & Advertising: The Art of Account Planning.
John Wiley & Sons, 1998.

Zyman, Sergio with Brott, Armin.
The End of Advertising As We Know It.
John Wiley & Sons, 2002.

INDEX